I0140339

Joseph and Aseneth
A Love Story

History, Text and Commentary

Joseph Lumpkin

Joseph Lumpkin

Joseph and Aseneth, A Love Story:
History, Text, and Commentary
Copyright © 2015 by Joseph B. Lumpkin
All rights reserved.

Printed in the United States of America. No part of this book may
be used or reproduced in any manner whatsoever without written
permission except in the case of brief quotations embodied in
critical articles and reviews.

Fifth Estate, Blountsville, AL 35031.

First Edition
Printed on acid-free paper

Library of Congress Control No: 2015902200
ISBN: 9781936533503

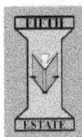

Fifth Estate, 2015

Table of Contents

Joseph Lumpkin

Preface

The story of Joseph and Aseneth is an epic story of love, desire, sanctification, and forgiveness. It is also a story of religious intolerance, racism, sexism, subterfuge, betrayal, and hate.

The story begins after Joseph's own brothers sold him into slavery. An Egyptian man purchased Joseph to be a servant to his wife. Because Joseph refused to serve her lustful desires, the woman had him thrown into prison on a false charge of rape. The Pharaoh, who saw greatness in him, pardoned Joseph and assigned him a position of power. Joseph, the ever-devout Jew, begins his new career living in a world of polytheists where he seems to be tolerated with more grace than he gives to those "abominations" who are neither Jewish in the racial or religious sense.

Aseneth is the daughter of the chief priest of the sun god. She is a spoiled, arrogant child who disdains all men, and even disrespects her father. Aseneth is cursed with beauty, which draws men to her like flies to a carnivorous plant. Even the son of Pharaoh wants her for himself and plots to get her. But Aseneth loathes and despises men, until she sees Joseph, who refuses to even touch her because she does not worship the same god as he. It is within this setting we begin the tale of Joseph and Aseneth.

The main text of the following chapter, History and Introduction, will be in plain font. Scriptural references will be placed in italicized font.

History and Introduction

The text of Joseph and Aseneth is an expansion of the biblical account contained in Genesis. The story itself it written as a narrative. The writing style is direct and clear, and at times rather simplistic. The names and places used in the Septuagint version of the Old testament seem to have more in common with the text than any other Bible version, but for the sake of a complete and comprehensive overview we shall look into the Bible translations of the New Living Translation and the Homan Christian Translation, and compare those with the Septuagint translation of Genesis.

The back-story of Joseph and Aseneth (or Asenath) begins in Genesis, chapters 37 - 41 where we see Joseph, an Israelite, sold into slavery by his brothers, bought by Ishmaelite traders, and resold into slavery to Potiphar, an Egyptian ruler under Pharaoh. Joseph is used as a house slave until the wife of Potiphar demands sexual attention from Joseph, which he declines to give. She turns the tables on Joseph, claiming he was the one who attempted to assault her. Potiphar, her husband, exacts justice and Joseph is condemned to a dungeon until the Pharaoh has a series of dreams, which only Joseph could interpret.

When Pharaoh has a dream, which seems to haunt him, Joseph is called upon to interpret the dream. The insight from the interpretation could save the nation. To implement the dream and institute the needed steps to save Egypt, Joseph is promoted from prisoner to Pharaoh's right-hand man (first man). Along with the promotion comes a wife of suitable stature. According to Genesis, Joseph is given Aseneth to wed. However, as we shall see in the story of Joseph and Aseneth, Joseph was not her first choice for a husband, nor was she his choice for a perfect bride.

The book of Joseph and Aseneth was written to "flesh out" and expand on the story of their meeting and engagement and put to rest problems seen by the Jews within the story. Not the least of which was how the noble Jew, Joseph, could marry an argumentative, self-willed, non-Jewish woman who was the daughter of a pagan priest. In a beginning resembling Shakespeare's "The Taming of the Shrew", Aseneth's heart is turned from rebellious to amorous. After falling in love with Joseph, she realizes her mistakes and asks God for help. As we shall see, God purified Aseneth's heart, making her a spiritual Jew, and uniting them in a holy covenant. Let us begin with the story as told by Genesis.

In Genesis 37 Joseph is sold into slavery by his brothers. They then go to their father, Jacob, and tell him Joseph was killed by a wild animal. The story picks up again in Genesis 39 as the captors that he was sold to arrive in Egypt and sell him again, this time to an Egyptian official.

Genesis 37 Holman Christian Bible
12 His brothers had gone to pasture their father's flocks at Shechem.
13 Israel said to Joseph, "Your brothers, you know, are pasturing the flocks at Shechem. Get ready. I'm sending you to them."
"I'm ready," Joseph replied.
14 Then Israel said to him, "Go and see how your brothers and the flocks are doing, and bring word back to me." So he sent him from the Valley of Hebron, and he went to Shechem.
15 A man found him there, wandering in the field, and asked him, "What are you looking for?"
16 "I'm looking for my brothers," Joseph said. "Can you tell me where they are pasturing their flocks?"

17 *"They've moved on from here," the man said. "I heard them say, 'Let's go to Dothan.'" So Joseph set out after his brothers and found them at Dothan.*

18 *They saw him in the distance, and before he had reached them, they plotted to kill him.* 19 *They said to one another, "Here comes that dreamer![b]* 20 *Come on, let's kill him and throw him into one of the pits. We can say that a vicious animal ate him. Then we'll see what becomes of his dreams!"*

21 *When Reuben heard this, he tried to save him from them.[c] He said, "Let's not take his life."* 22 *Reuben also said to them, "Don't shed blood. Throw him into this pit in the wilderness, but don't lay a hand on him" – intending to rescue him from their hands and return him to his father.*

23 *When Joseph came to his brothers, they stripped off his robe, the robe of many colors that he had on.* 24 *Then they took him and threw him into the pit. The pit was empty; there was no water in it.*

25 *Then they sat down to eat a meal. They looked up, and there was a caravan of Ishmaelites coming from Gilead. Their camels were carrying aromatic gum, balsam, and resin, going down to Egypt.* 26 *Then Judah said to his brothers, "What do we gain if we kill our brother and cover up his blood?* 27 *Come, let's sell him to the Ishmaelites and not lay a hand on him, for he is our brother, our own flesh," and they agreed.* 28 *When Midianite traders passed by, his brothers pulled Joseph out of the pit and sold him for 20 pieces of silver to the Ishmaelites, who took Joseph to Egypt.*

29 *When Reuben returned to the pit and saw that Joseph was not there, he tore his clothes. 30 He went back to his brothers and said, "The boy is gone! What am I going to do?"[d] 31 So they took Joseph's robe, slaughtered a young goat, and dipped the robe in its blood. 32 They sent the robe of many colors to their father and said, "We found this. Examine it. Is it your son's robe or not?"*

33 His father recognized it. "It is my son's robe," he said. "A vicious animal has devoured him. Joseph has been torn to pieces!" 34 Then Jacob tore his clothes, put sackcloth around his waist, and mourned for his son many days. 35 All his sons and daughters tried to comfort him, but he refused to be comforted. "No," he said. "I will go down to Sheol to my son, mourning." And his father wept for him. 36 Meanwhile, the Midianites sold Joseph in Egypt to Potiphar, an officer of Pharaoh and the captain of the guard.

Footnotes:

Genesis 37:3 Or robe with long sleeves

Genesis 37:19 Lit comes the lord of the dreams

Genesis 37:21 Lit their hands

Genesis 37:30 Lit And I, where am I going

Genesis 39 New Living Translation (NLT)

Joseph in Potiphar's House

39 *When Joseph was taken to Egypt by the Ishmaelite traders, he was purchased by Potiphar, an Egyptian officer. Potiphar was captain of the guard for Pharaoh, the king of Egypt.*

2 The Lord was with Joseph, so he succeeded in everything he did as he served in the home of his Egyptian master. 3 Potiphar noticed this and realized that the Lord was with Joseph, giving him success in everything he did. 4 This pleased Potiphar, so he soon made Joseph his personal attendant. He put him in charge of his entire household and everything he owned. 5 From the day Joseph was put in charge of his master's household and property, the Lord began to bless Potiphar's household for Joseph's sake. All his household affairs ran smoothly, and his crops and livestock flourished. 6 So Potiphar gave Joseph complete administrative responsibility over everything he owned. With Joseph there, he didn't worry about a thing — except what kind of food to eat!

Joseph was a very handsome and well-built young man, 7 and Potiphar's wife soon began to look at him lustfully. "Come and sleep with me," she demanded.

8 But Joseph refused. "Look," he told her, "my master trusts me with everything in his entire household. 9 No one here has more authority than I do. He has held back nothing from me except you, because you are his wife. How could I do such a wicked thing? It would be a great sin against God."

10 She kept putting pressure on Joseph day after day, but he refused to sleep with her, and he kept out of her way as much as possible. 11

One day, however, no one else was around when he went in to do his work. 12 She came and grabbed him by his cloak, demanding, "Come on, sleep with me!" Joseph tore himself away, but he left his cloak in her hand as he ran from the house.

13 When she saw that she was holding his cloak and he had fled, 14 she called out to her servants. Soon all the men came running. "Look!" she said. "My husband has brought this Hebrew slave here to make fools of us! He came into my room to rape me, but I screamed. 15 When he heard me scream, he ran outside and got away, but he left his cloak behind with me."

16 She kept the cloak with her until her husband came home. 17 Then she told him her story. "That Hebrew slave you've brought into our house tried to come in and fool around with me," she said. 18 "But when I screamed, he ran outside, leaving his cloak with me!"

Joseph Put in Prison

19 Potiphar was furious when he heard his wife's story about how Joseph had treated her. 20 So he took Joseph and threw him into the prison where the king's prisoners were held, and there he remained. 21 But the Lord was with Joseph in the prison and showed him his faithful love. And the Lord made Joseph a favorite with the prison warden. 22 Before long, the warden put Joseph in charge of all the other prisoners and over everything that happened in the prison. 23 The warden had no more worries, because Joseph took care of

everything. The Lord was with him and caused everything he did to
succeed.

Genesis 40 New Living Translation (NLT)
Joseph Interprets Two Dreams
40 Some time later, Pharaoh's chief cup-bearer and chief baker
offended their royal master. 2 Pharaoh became angry with these two
officials, 3 and he put them in the prison where Joseph was, in the
palace of the captain of the guard. 4 They remained in prison for
quite some time, and the captain of the guard assigned them to
Joseph, who looked after them.
5 While they were in prison, Pharaoh's cup-bearer and baker each
had a dream one night, and each dream had its own meaning. 6
When Joseph saw them the next morning, he noticed that they both
looked upset. 7 "Why do you look so worried today?" he asked them.
8 And they replied, "We both had dreams last night, but no one can
tell us what they mean."
"Interpreting dreams is God's business," Joseph replied. "Go ahead
and tell me your dreams."
9 So the chief cup-bearer told Joseph his dream first. "In my dream,"
he said, "I saw a grapevine in front of me. 10 The vine had three
branches that began to bud and blossom, and soon it produced
clusters of ripe grapes. 11 I was holding Pharaoh's wine cup in my
hand, so I took a cluster of grapes and squeezed the juice into the
cup. Then I placed the cup in Pharaoh's hand."

12 *"This is what the dream means," Joseph said. "The three branches represent three days. 13 Within three days Pharaoh will lift you up and restore you to your position as his chief cup-bearer. 14 And please remember me and do me a favor when things go well for you. Mention me to Pharaoh, so he might let me out of this place. 15 For I was kidnapped from my homeland, the land of the Hebrews, and now I'm here in prison, but I did nothing to deserve it."*

16 *When the chief baker saw that Joseph had given the first dream such a positive interpretation, he said to Joseph, "I had a dream, too. In my dream there were three baskets of white pastries stacked on my head. 17 The top basket contained all kinds of pastries for Pharaoh, but the birds came and ate them from the basket on my head."*

18 *"This is what the dream means," Joseph told him. "The three baskets also represent three days. 19 Three days from now Pharaoh will lift you up and impale your body on a pole. Then birds will come and peck away at your flesh."*

20 *Pharaoh's birthday came three days later, and he prepared a banquet for all his officials and staff. He summoned [a] his chief cup-bearer and chief baker to join the other officials. 21 He then restored the chief cup-bearer to his former position, so he could again hand Pharaoh his cup. 22 But Pharaoh impaled the chief baker, just as Joseph had predicted when he interpreted his dream. 23 Pharaoh's chief cup-bearer, however, forgot all about Joseph, never giving him another thought.*

Footnotes:

40:20 Hebrew He lifted up the head of.

Genesis 41 New Living Translation (NLT)

Pharaoh's Dreams

41 Two full years later, Pharaoh dreamed that he was standing on the bank of the Nile River. 2 In his dream he saw seven fat, healthy cows come up out of the river and begin grazing in the marsh grass. 3 Then he saw seven more cows come up behind them from the Nile, but these were scrawny and thin. These cows stood beside the fat cows on the riverbank. 4 Then the scrawny, thin cows ate the seven healthy, fat cows! At this point in the dream, Pharaoh woke up.

5 But he fell asleep again and had a second dream. This time he saw seven heads of grain, plump and beautiful, growing on a single stalk. 6 Then seven more heads of grain appeared, but these were shriveled and withered by the east wind. 7 And these thin heads swallowed up the seven plump, well-formed heads! Then Pharaoh woke up again and realized it was a dream.

8 The next morning Pharaoh was very disturbed by the dreams. So he called for all the magicians and wise men of Egypt. When Pharaoh told them his dreams, not one of them could tell him what they meant.

9 Finally, the king's chief cup-bearer spoke up. "Today I have been reminded of my failure," he told Pharaoh. 10 "Some time ago, you were angry with the chief baker and me, and you imprisoned us in the palace of the captain of the guard. 11 One night the chief baker and I each had a dream, and each dream had its own meaning. 12 There was a young Hebrew man with us in the prison who was a slave of the captain of the guard. We told him our dreams, and he told us what each of our dreams meant. 13 And everything happened just as he had predicted. I was restored to my position as cup-bearer, and the chief baker was executed and impaled on a pole."

14 Pharaoh sent for Joseph at once, and he was quickly brought from the prison. After he shaved and changed his clothes, he went in and stood before Pharaoh. 15 Then Pharaoh said to Joseph, "I had a dream last night, and no one here can tell me what it means. But I have heard that when you hear about a dream you can interpret it."

16 "It is beyond my power to do this," Joseph replied. "But God can tell you what it means and set you at ease."

17 So Pharaoh told Joseph his dream. "In my dream," he said, "I was standing on the bank of the Nile River, 18 and I saw seven fat, healthy cows come up out of the river and begin grazing in the marsh grass. 19 But then I saw seven sick-looking cows, scrawny and thin, come up after them. I've never seen such sorry-looking animals in all the land of Egypt. 20 These thin, scrawny cows ate the seven fat cows. 21 But afterward you wouldn't have known it, for they were still as thin and scrawny as before! Then I woke up.

22 "In my dream I also saw seven heads of grain, full and beautiful, growing on a single stalk. 23 Then seven more heads of grain appeared, but these were blighted, shriveled, and withered by the east wind. 24 And the shriveled heads swallowed the seven healthy heads. I told these dreams to the magicians, but no one could tell me what they mean."

25 Joseph responded, "Both of Pharaoh's dreams mean the same thing. God is telling Pharaoh in advance what he is about to do. 26 The seven healthy cows and the seven healthy heads of grain both represent seven years of prosperity. 27 The seven thin, scrawny cows that came up later and the seven thin heads of grain, withered by the east wind, represent seven years of famine.

28 "This will happen just as I have described it, for God has revealed to Pharaoh in advance what he is about to do. 29 The next seven years will be a period of great prosperity throughout the land of Egypt. 30 But afterward there will be seven years of famine so great that all the prosperity will be forgotten in Egypt. Famine will destroy the land. 31 This famine will be so severe that even the memory of the good years will be erased. 32 As for having two similar dreams, it means that these events have been decreed by God, and he will soon make them happen.

33 "Therefore, Pharaoh should find an intelligent and wise man and put him in charge of the entire land of Egypt. 34 Then Pharaoh should appoint supervisors over the land and let them collect one-fifth of all the crops during the seven good years. 35 Have them gather all the food produced in the good years that are just ahead and bring it to Pharaoh's storehouses. Store it away, and guard it so there will be food in the cities. 36 That way there will be enough to

*eat when the seven years of famine come to the land of Egypt.
Otherwise this famine will destroy the land."*

Joseph Made Ruler of Egypt

*37 Joseph's suggestions were well received by Pharaoh and his
officials. 38 So Pharaoh asked his officials, "Can we find anyone else
like this man so obviously filled with the spirit of God?" 39 Then
Pharaoh said to Joseph, "Since God has revealed the meaning of the
dreams to you, clearly no one else is as intelligent or wise as you are.
40 You will be in charge of my court, and all my people will take
orders from you. Only I, sitting on my throne, will have a rank
higher than yours."*

*41 Pharaoh said to Joseph, "I hereby put you in charge of the entire
land of Egypt." 42 Then Pharaoh removed his signet ring from his
hand and placed it on Joseph's finger. He dressed him in fine linen
clothing and hung a gold chain around his neck. 43 Then he had
Joseph ride in the chariot reserved for his second-in-command. And
wherever Joseph went, the command was shouted, "Kneel down!" So
Pharaoh put Joseph in charge of all Egypt. 44 And Pharaoh said to
him, "I am Pharaoh, but no one will lift a hand or foot in the entire
land of Egypt without your approval."*

*45 Then Pharaoh gave Joseph a new Egyptian name, Zaphenath-
paneah.[a] He also gave him a wife, whose name was Asenath. She
was the daughter of Potiphera, the priest of On.[b] So Joseph took
charge of the entire land of Egypt. 46 He was thirty years old when*

he began serving in the court of Pharaoh, the king of Egypt. And
when Joseph left Pharaoh's presence, he inspected the entire land of
Egypt.

47 As predicted, for seven years the land produced bumper crops. 48
During those years, Joseph gathered all the crops grown in Egypt
and stored the grain from the surrounding fields in the cities. 49 He
piled up huge amounts of grain like sand on the seashore. Finally, he
stopped keeping records because there was too much to measure.

50 During this time, before the first of the famine years, two sons
were born to Joseph and his wife, Asenath, the daughter of Potiphera,
the priest of On. 51 Joseph named his older son Manasseh,[c] for he
said, "God has made me forget all my troubles and everyone in my
father's family." 52 Joseph named his second son Ephraim,[d] for he
said, "God has made me fruitful in this land of my grief."

53 At last the seven years of bumper crops throughout the land of
Egypt came to an end. 54 Then the seven years of famine began, just
as Joseph had predicted. The famine also struck all the surrounding
countries, but throughout Egypt there was plenty of food. 55
Eventually, however, the famine spread throughout the land of
Egypt as well. And when the people cried out to Pharaoh for food, he
told them, "Go to Joseph, and do whatever he tells you." 56 So with
severe famine everywhere, Joseph opened up the storehouses and
distributed grain to the Egyptians, for the famine was severe
throughout the land of Egypt. 57 And people from all around came

to Egypt to buy grain from Joseph because the famine was severe throughout the world.

Footnotes:
41:45a Zaphenath-paneah probably means "God speaks and lives."
41:45b Greek version reads of Heliopolis; also in 41:50.
41:51 Manasseh sounds like a Hebrew term that means "causing to forget."
41:52 Ephraim sounds like a Hebrew term that means "fruitful."
New Living Translation (NLT)
Holy Bible. New Living Translation copyright© 1996, 2004, 2007, 2013 by Tyndale House Foundation.

There is ongoing debate as to whether Potiphar and Potipherah are the same person. The names are essentially the same, or at least close variants of the same root name. Yet, for the story to have the needed continuity the names should be treated as different and belonging to different men. Just as Mary and Maria have the same root but could be assigned to different women, so could the names of Potiphar and Potipherah belong to different individuals.

Potiphar is identified in Genesis 39 as: Potiphar, an officer of Pharaoh, captain of the guard, an Egyptian. This Potipar is also identified in some translations as a eunuch.

Genesis 39 1599 Geneva Bible (GNV)
1 Now Joseph was brought down into Egypt: and Potiphar an Eunuch of Pharaoh's (and his chief steward an Egyptian) bought him at the hand of the Ishmaelites, which had brought him thither.

Being a eunuch, the officer would father no children and have no daughter. It must be mentioned that the translation of the word "eunuch" has been dropped by most translations and replaced with "officer" and "chief executioner", however, if the translation is true it would certainly put to rest the debate.

Genesis 39 Amplified Bible (AMP)
39 And Joseph was brought down to Egypt; and Potiphar, an officer of Pharaoh, the captain and chief executioner of the [royal] guard, an Egyptian, bought him from the Ishmaelites who had brought him down there.

Potipherah, mentioned in Genesis 41 is: Poti-pherah priest of the city of On. The city of On is the Biblical name of the Greek city of Heliopolis.

The story line would twist and turn on itself if Potipher, whose wife tried desperately to seduce Joseph and when denied her lust vengefully had him thrown in prison, were to watch without a word as Joseph married her daughter. This contradiction would not work well within human nature. It is far more likely that the story contains two men with similar names, one of whom is an officer and one a priest.

The idea of two men of similar names and different vocations is tidy but all comes into doubt when the Septuagint is examined, for there the names are identical and a new approach is called for. We are left with more questions than answers as we try to make sense of the story and all of its ramifications. Did Potipherah, now called Petephres in the Septuagint, turn from the Pharaoh's officer and retire to become the priest of Ra? It is not impossible. Did the wife of Petephres manage to keep her wits about her and her mouth closed as the Pharaoh gave her daughter to the man who rejected her? Did she swallow her pride in order to see her daughter wed to the second most powerful man in Egypt? If the two men named Petephres mentioned in the Septuagint are the same person there is an awkward silence about the false charges and time in prison thrust on Joseph by this man and his lying wife.

The answer to these questions could reside in the fact that the subtle differences in the two names were lost during the transliteration of Potiphar and Potipherah from Hebrew into Greek as the names were rendered for use in the Septuagint.

POTIPHAR (פּוֹטִיפַר) or POTI-PHERAH (פּוֹטִי פֶרַע):

Name of an Egyptian officer. The form "Potiphar" is probably
an abbreviation of "Potiphera"; the two are treated as identical
in the Septuagint, and are rendered Πετρεφῆς or Πετεφῆς.
"Poti-phera" is the Hebrew rendering of the Egyptian "P'-di-p'-
R'" = "He whom Ra [i.e., the sun-god] gave." This name has not
been found in Egyptian inscriptions; but names of similar
form occur as early as the twenty-second dynasty.
Potiphar was the Egyptian officer to whom Joseph was sold
(Gen. xxxvii. 36, xxxix. 1). He is described as a "saris" of
Pharaoh, and as "captain of the guard" (Hebr. שַׂר הַטַּבָּחִים).
The term "saris" is commonly used in the Old Testament of
eunuchs; but occasionally it seems to stand in a more general
sense for "court official," and sometimes it designates a
military officer (II Kings xxv. 19; comp. ib. xviii. 17; Jer. xxxix.
3, 13). The second title, "captain of the guard," is literally "chief
of the slaughterers," and is interpreted by some to mean "chief
of the cooks" (comp. I Sam. ix. 23, 24, where טַבָּח = "cook").
The former is much the more probable meaning here, and is
supported by the closely corresponding title (רַב טַבָּחִים) of
one of the high military officers of Nebuchadnezzar (II Kings

xxv. 8, 10; comp. Dan. ii. 14). Nothing, however, of this office is definitely known from Egyptian sources.

Poti-pherah was a priest of On (Heliopolis), whose daughter Asenath became the wife of Joseph (Gen. xli. 45, 50; xlvi. 20). See also Joseph.

(Jewish Encyclopedia)

The Septuagint does not attempt to make any distinction between the two men accept for explaining that they had separate job descriptions. We are not told where the first Petephres resided, but it was likely where the Pharaoh was housed. The second man lived in Heliopolis.

Septuagint

Genesis 39:1 And Joseph was brought down to Egypt; and Petephres the eunuch of Pharao, the captain of the guard, an Egyptian, bought him of the hands of the Ismaelites, who brought him down thither. 2 And the Lord was with Joseph, and he was a prosperous man; and he was in the house with his lord the Egyptian. 3 And his master knew that the Lord was with him, and the Lord prospers in his hands whatsoever he happens to do. 4 And Joseph found grace in the presence of his lord, and was well-pleasing to him; and he set him over his house, and all that he had he gave into the hand of Joseph. 5 And it came to pass after that he was set over his house, and over all that he had, that the Lord blessed the house of the Egyptian for Joseph's sake; and the blessing of the Lord was on all his possessions in the house, and in his field. 6 And he committed all that he had into the hands of Joseph; and he knew not of anything that belonged to him, save the bread which he himself ate. And Joseph was handsome in form, and exceedingly beautiful in countenance. 7 And it came to pass after these things, that his master's wife cast her eyes upon Joseph, and said, Lie with me. 8 But he would not; but said to his master's wife, If because of me my master knows nothing in his house, and has given into my hands all things that belong to him: 9 and in this house there is nothing above me, nor has anything been kept back from me, but thou, because thou art his wife — how then shall I do this wicked thing, and sin against God? 10 And when she talked with Joseph day by day, and he hearkened not to her to sleep with her, so as to be with her, 11 it came to pass on a certain day, that Joseph went into the house to do his business, and there was no one of the household within. 12 And she caught hold of him by his clothes, and said, Lie with me; and having left his clothes in her hands, he fled, and went forth. 13 And it came to pass, when she saw that he had left his clothes in her hands, and fled, and gone forth, 14 that she called those that were in the house, and spoke to them, saying, See, he has brought in to us a Hebrew servant to mock us — he came in to me, saying, Lie with me, and I cried with a loud voice. 15 And when he heard that I lifted up my voice and cried, having left his clothes with me, he fled, and went forth out. 16 So she leaves the clothes by her, until the master came to his house. 17 And she spoke to him according to these words, saying, The Hebrew servant, whom thou broughtest in to us, came in to me to mock me, and said to me, I will lie with thee. 18 And when he heard that I lifted up my voice and cried, having left his clothes with me, he fled and departed forth. 19 And it came to pass, when his master heard all the words of his wife, that she spoke to him, saying, Thus did thy servant to me, that he was very angry.

20 And his master took Joseph, and cast him into the prison, into the place where the king's prisoners are kept, there in the prison. 21 And the Lord was with Joseph, and poured down mercy upon him; and he gave him favour in the sight of the chief keeper of the prison. 22 And the chief keeper of the prison gave the prison into the hand of Joseph, and all the prisoners as many as were in the prison; and all things whatsoever they do there, he did them. 23 Because of him the chief keeper of the prison knew nothing, for all things were in the hand of Joseph, because the Lord was with him; and whatever things he did, the Lord made them to prosper in his hands.

40:1 And it came to pass after these things, that the chief cupbearer of the king of Egypt and the chief baker trespassed against their lord the king of Egypt. 2 And Pharao was wroth with his two eunuchs, with his chief cupbearer, and with his chief baker. 3 And he put them in ward, into the prison, into the place whereinto Joseph had been led. 4 And the chief keeper of the prison committed them to Joseph, and he stood by them; and they were some days in the prison. 5 And they both had a dream in one night; and the vision of the dream of the chief cupbearer and chief baker, who belonged to the king of Egypt, who were in the prison, was this. 6 Joseph went in to them in the morning, and saw them, and they had been troubled. 7 And he asked the eunuchs of Pharao who were with him in the prison with his master, saying, Why is it that your countenances are sad to-day? 8 And they said to him, We have seen a dream, and there is no interpreter of it. And Joseph said to them, Is not the interpretation of them through god? tell them than to me. 9 And the chief cupbearer related his dream to Joseph, and said, In my dream a vine was before me. 10 And in the vine were three stems; and it budding shot forth blossoms; the clusters of grapes were ripe. 11 And the cup of Pharao was in my hand; and I took the bunch of grapes, and squeezed it into the cup, and gave the cup into Pharao's hand. 12 And Joseph said to him, This is the interpretation of it. The three stems are three days. 13 Yet three days and Pharao shall remember thy office, and he shall restore thee to thy place of chief cupbearer, and thou shalt give the cup of Pharao into his hand, according to thy former high place, as thou wast wont to be cupbearer. 14 But remember me of thyself, when it shall be well with thee, and thou shalt deal mercifully with me, and thou shalt make mention of me to Pharao, and thou shalt bring me forth out of this dungeon. 15 For surely I was stolen away out of the land of the Hebrews, and here I have done nothing, but *they have cast me into this pit. 16 And the chief baker saw that he interpreted aright; and he said to Joseph, I also saw a dream, and methought I took up on my head three baskets of mealy food. 17 And in the upper basket there was the work of the baker of every kind which Pharao eats; and the fowls of the air ate them out of the basket that was on my head. 18 And Joseph answered and said to him, This is the interpretation of it; The three baskets are three days. 19 Yet three days, and Pharao shall take away thy head from off thee, and shall hang thee on a tree, and the birds of the sky shall eat thy flesh from off thee. 20 And it came to pass on the third day that it was Pharao's birth-day, and he made a banquet for all his servants, and he remembered the office of the cupbearer and the office of the baker in the midst of his servants. 21 And he restored the chief cupbearer to his office, and he gave the cup into Pharao's hand. 22 And he hanged the chief baker, as Joseph, interpreted to them. 23 Yet did not the chief cupbearer remember Joseph, but forgot him.*

41:1 And it came to pass after two full years that Pharao had a dream. He thought he stood upon the bank of the river. 2 And lo, there came up as it were out of the river seven cows, fair in appearance, and choice of flesh, and they fed on the sedge. 3 And other seven cows came up after these out of the river, ill-favoured and lean-fleshed, and fed by the other cows on the bank of the river. 4 And the seven ill-favoured and lean cows devoured the seven well-

favoured and choice-fleshed cows; and Pharao awoke. 5 And he dreamed again. And, behold, seven ears came up on one stalk, choice and good. 6 And, behold, seven ears thin and blasted with the wind, grew up after them. 7 And the seven thin ears and blasted with the wind devoured the seven choice and full ears; and Pharao awoke, and it was a dream. 8 And it was morning, and his soul was troubled; and he sent and called all the interpreters of Egypt, and all her wise men; and Pharao related to them his dream, and there was no one to interpret it to Pharao. 9 And the chief cupbearer spoke to Pharao, saying, I this day remember my fault: 10 Pharao was angry with his servants, and put us in prison in the house of the captain of the guard, both me and the chief baker. 11 And we had a dream both in one night, I and he; we saw, each according to his dream. 12 And there was there with us a young man, a Hebrew servant of the captain of the guard; and we related to him our dreams, and he interpreted them to us. 13 And it came to pass, as he interpreted them to us, so also it happened, both that I was restored to my office, and that he was hanged. 14 And Pharao having sent, called Joseph; and they brought him out from the prison, and shaved him, and changed his dress, and he came to Pharao. 15 And Pharao said to Joseph, I have seen a vision, and there is no one to interpret it; but I have heard say concerning thee that thou didst hear dreams and interpret them. 16 And Joseph answered Pharao and said, Without God an answer of safety shall not be given to Pharao. 17 And Pharao spoke to Joseph, saying, In my dream methought I stood by the bank of the river; 18 and there came up as it were out of the river, seven cows well-favoured and choice-fleshed, and they fed on the sedge. 19 And behold seven other cows came up after them out of the river, evil and ill-favoured and lean-fleshed, such that I never saw worse in all the land of Egypt. 20 And the seven ill-favoured and thin cows ate up the seven first good and choice cows. 21 And they went into their bellies; and it was not perceptible that they had gone into their bellies, and their appearance was ill-favoured, as also at the beginning; and after I awoke I slept, 22 and saw again in my sleep, and as it were seven ears came up on one stem, full and good. 23 And other seven ears, thin and blasted with the wind, sprang up close to them. 24 And the seven thin and blasted ears devoured the seven fine and full ears: so I spoke to the interpreters, and there was no one to explain it to me.

25 And Joseph said to Pharao, The dream of Pharao is one; whatever God does, he has shewn to Pharao. 26 The seven good cows are seven years, and the seven good ears are seven years; the dream of Pharao is one. 27 And the seven thin kine that came up after them are seven years; and the seven thin and blasted ears are seven years; there shall be seven years of famine. 28 And as for the word which I have told Pharao, whatsoever God intends to do, he has shewn to Pharao: 29 behold, for seven years there is coming great plenty in all the land of Egypt. 30 But there shall come seven years of famine after these, and they shall forget the plenty that shall be in all Egypt, and the famine shall consume the land. 31 And the plenty shall not be known in the land by reason of the famine that shall be after this, for it shall be very grievous. 32 And concerning the repetition of the dream to Pharao twice, it is because the saying which is from God shall be true, and God will hasten to accomplish it. 33 Now then, look out a wise and prudent man, and set him over the land of Egypt. 34 And let Pharao make and appoint local governors over the land; and let them take up a fifth part of all the produce of the land of Egypt for the seven years of the plenty. 35 And let them gather all the food of these seven good years that are coming, and let the corn be gathered under the hand of Pharao; let food be kept in the cities. 36 And the stored food shall be for the land against the seven years of famine, which shall be in the land of Egypt; and the land shall not be utterly destroyed by the famine. 37 And the word was pleasing in the sight of Pharao, and in the sight of all his servants.

38 And Pharao said to all his servants, Shall we find such a man as this, who has the Spirit of God in him? 39 And Pharao said to Joseph, Since God has shewed thee all these things, there is not a wiser or more prudent man than thou. 40 Thou shalt be over my house, and all my people shall be obedient to thy word; only in the throne will I excel thee. 41 And Pharao said to Joseph, Behold, I set thee this day over all the land of Egypt. 42 And Pharao took his ring off his hand, and put it on the hand of Joseph, and put on him a robe of fine linen, and put a necklace of gold about his neck. 43 And he

*mounted him on the second of his chariots, and a herald made
proclamation before him; and he set him over all the land of Egypt.
44 And Pharao said to Joseph, I am Pharao; without thee no one
shall lift up his hand on all the land of Egypt. 45 And Pharao called
the name of Joseph, Psonthomphanech; and he gave him Aseneth, the
daughter of Petephres, priest of Heliopolis, to wife. 46 And Joseph
was thirty years old when he stood before Pharao, king of Egypt.
And Joseph went out from the presence of Pharao, and went through
all the land of Egypt. 47 And the land produced, in the seven years
of plenty, whole handfuls of corn. 48 And he gathered all the food of
the seven years, in which was the plenty in the land of Egypt; and he
laid up the food in the cities; the food of the fields of a city round
about it he laid up in it. 49 And Joseph gathered very much corn as
the sand of the sea, until it could not be numbered, for there was no
number of it.*

*50 And to Joseph were born two sons, before the seven years of
famine came, which Aseneth, the daughter of Petephres, priest of
Heliopolis, bore to him. 51 And Joseph called the name of the first-
born, Manasse; for God, said he, has made me forget all my toils, and
all my father's house. 52 And he called the name of the second,
Ephraim; for God, said he, has increased me in the land of my
humiliation. 53 And the seven years of plenty passed away, which
were in the land of Egypt. 54 And the seven years of famine began to
come, as Joseph said; and there was a famine in all the land; but in*

all the land of Egypt there was bread. 55 And all the land of Egypt
was hungry; and the people cried to Pharao for bread. And Pharao
said to all the Egyptians, Go to Joseph, and do whatsoever he shall
tell you. 56 And the famine was on the face of all the earth; and
Joseph opened all the granaries, and sold to all the Egyptians. 57
And all countries came to Egypt to buy of Joseph, for the famine
prevailed in all the earth.

For the sake of story continuity and for the story to align with
basic human nature, we will look at these men with the same
name as different people. The first man called Petephres was
an officer. The second was a priest. The fact that Petephres or
Potipherah was the head priest in Heliopolis is no small issue.
The inhabitance of the city worshipped many gods, with the
major god being the sun-god Ra, also identified with Atum or
Atum-Ra.

This brings us to one of the reasons the book of Joseph and
Aseneth was written. The story of Joseph, as told in the Old
Testament, is an affront to later Jewish practice and brings up
many questions. How could Joseph, a passionately pious Jew,
marry the daughter of a pagan priest? How could Joseph go to
prison in defense of his faith and honor and then throw it to
the wind to marry a non-Jew?

When a book or text is written for the purpose of expanding the narrative in order to teach or explain the Biblical text the resultant work is called Midrash

Midrash is an interpretive act, seeking to answers practical and theological religious questions by exploring the meaning of the words of the Torah. Sometimes this results in stories which are speculative in nature but whose narrative would put to rest questions or conflicts left unaddressed within the biblical text.

In the Bible, the root d-r-sh is used to mean inquiring into any matter, including God's word. Midrash responds to contemporary problems and crafts new stories connecting new Jewish realities, beliefs, or laws with the biblical text being examined.

Dating the text of Joseph and Aseneth is controversial, to say the least. Noted scholars have greatly varying views as to dates and geographical origins.

The work is anonymous. The dating is contentious, and it is not even clear whether this is a Jewish or a Christian work, although the core of the texts seems to be Jewish, since it seems to have been written to clear up concerns left by the brevity of the original story in the Torah. However, Batiffol (who produced the first critical edition) and, more recently, Kraemer have argued that it was originally a Christian work, dating from the fourth or fifth centuries. Kraemer suggests connections with works like Acts of Thomas.

Rivka Nir, of the Open University of Israel states: The pseudepigraphic work Joseph and Aseneth consists of two main stories. The first part of the work, which is also the longest (chs. 1– 21), relates the love story between the two protagonists, Aseneth's conversion, and her marriage with Joseph. It is followed by a shorter story (chs. 22–29) narrating the unsuccessful attempt by Pharaoh's son—who is assisted by some of Joseph's brothers—to abduct Aseneth and make her his wife. It is agreed that the story was originally composed in Greek. There are 16 Greek manuscripts, dating from the 10th to the 19th centuries, which can be divided into two groups: a shorter text, published by M. Philonenko, Joseph et Aseneth: Introduction, texte critique, traduction et notes (StPB, 13; Leiden: Brill, 1968), on which D. Cook based the English translation "Joseph and Aseneth," in H. F. D. Sparks (ed.), The Apocryphal Old Testament (Oxford: Clarendon Press, 1984), 473–503; and a longer text published by C. Burchard, Untersuchungen zu Joseph und Aseneth: Überlieferung

– Ortsbestimmung (WUNT, 8; Tübingen: Mohr, 1965), and idem, Joseph und

Aseneth (Leiden: Brill, 2003). The story in chs. 22–29 was composed by a Christian author, and with a Christian audience in view. At the center of the story is a call for Christians to adopt an ethics characterized by non-retaliation and the love of enemies as a means to obtain salvation in the Church, itself personified by Aseneth.

Klassen dismisses possible Christian interpolations, "for nothing is found in this story which is unique to Christian sources; indeed it would be hard to find anything here which is clearly stated in the New Testament." Similarly, Zerbe concludes that, "the ethic of non-retaliation in Joseph and Aseneth then, is inspired primarily by biblical texts and traditions."

Thus, with the greatest scholars of the day divided about dates and religious origin, and with the observation of the existence of two separate divisions or stories within Joseph and Aseneth, we are left wondering about when and why the text was written, or if indeed the two parts of the text have their own authors, dates, and reasons for existence.

The earliest version is in Syriac and dates from the sixth century AD. Most modern scholarship treats it as a Jewish work dating some time from first century BC to the second AD.

Early versions exist today in Syriac, Slavonic, Armenian and Latin – but there is general consensus that it was originally composed in Greek.

Chr. Burchard writes: "JosAsen appears to have originated in the Jewish diaspora of Egypt, no later than c. AD 100 and perhaps as early as the first century BC. A sectarian milieu has been suggested: Essenes, Therapeutae, or some unknown form of Judaism shaped in the image of a Hellenistic mystery religion. But the book presents Judaism, not a special form distinct from others. According to some scholars, it was written to promote Jewish mission among non-Jews, or Jews, or both. However, Judaism as depicted in JosAsen is not mission-minded. Besides the book never bothers to explain Jewish life. The Sabbath, circumcision, the interdiction against pork, the standards of levitical purity, indeed the necessity of keeping the Law, which is fundamental to all forms of Judaism, go unmentioned. So it is safer to assume that JosAsen was meant to be read by Jews as a reminder of the supernatural vitality and lofty morality, which were theirs.

We should remember, however, that the Egyptian diaspora undoubtedly included many proselytes and attracted 'God-fearing' sympathizers such as we know, e.g., from the Book of Acts." (Outside the Old Testament, p. 94)

James Charlesworth writes: "That Joseph and Asenath is a fifth-century Christian work, based upon a Jewish writing, is a dated conclusion (P. Batiffol, Le Livre de la Prière d'Asénath [Studia Patristica 1-2] Paris: Leroux, 1889-1890). That it is an early, perhaps late first-century A.D., Jewish composition is a contemporary perspective (cf. C. Burchard, Untersuchungen zu Joseph und Aseneth. Tübingen: Mohr, 1965; see esp. pp. 148-51; Philonenko, no. 1003; A.-M. Denis, no. 24, pp. 40-48). Most scholars now contend that the original language is Greek (Burchard, Untersuch., pp. 91-99; Philonenko, no. 1003, pp. 27-32). The parallels with the Dead Sea Scrolls have raised the possibility of influence from the Essenes, or more probably from the Therapeutae; some scholars affirm a relationship (P. Riessler, no. 62, p. 1303; K. G. Kuhn in The Scrolls and the New Testament, ed. K. Stendhal. New York: Harper, 1957; pp. 75f.; M. Delcor, 'Un roman d'amour d'origine thérapeute: le livre de Joseph et Asénath,' BLE 63 [1962] 3-27); others deny it (Philonenko, no. 1003, p. 105; Burchard, Untersuch., pp. 107-12)." (The Pseudepigrapha and Modern Research, p. 137)

Mark Seitz of Northwest Nazarene University writes: Joseph and Aseneth is a narrative describing the conversion of Aseneth, the pagan wife of the patriarch Joseph. The story is set in Egypt when Joseph was gathering grain in preparation for future famine. Aseneth, the daughter of Pentephres the priest of Heliopolis , falls in love with the handsome Joseph. Joseph refuses to marry her because she worships idols. Only after Aseneth repents of her idols and converts to the worship of Joseph's God do they marry and conceive two sons. Joseph becomes the target of the envy of Pharaoh's son, who enlists the aid of some of Joseph's brothers. But Joseph's other brothers and God defend him. During the conspiracy, both Pharaoh and his son die, leaving Joseph to succeed to rule over all Egypt. The book's language and imagery of conversion has many similarities to that used in early Christianity.

This book attempts to explain and elaborate upon these Old Testament passages. Later Jewish sentiments considered exogamous marriages between Jews and pagans offensive. Author: anonymous. Possibly Jews of Essene or Therapeutae sects Possibly Egyptian Jews, with interpolations by anonymous Christians.

Date and Origin: Between the 1st century BC and early 2nd century AD probably Egypt

Original Language: Originally written in Greek Versions are extant in Armenian, Slavonic, Latin, Middle English, and Syriac.

As with many of the midrash texts, the storylines may start out as an attempt to explain inconvenient lapses in more modern Jewish customs or laws, but they sometimes end up in flights of fantasy, as with this one where the pagan Pharaoh and his evil son die, leaving Joseph to rule over Egypt, a fact left unaccounted for in any history book. Still, the impetus to write the story and explain the complications of marriage outside of the Jewish faith most certainly drove the heart of the story. For this reason it seems reasonable to assign a date in which a Jewish orthodoxy existed that would lead to such a work as this text. The Essene community would be a possible origin, but if the text was first written in Greek these pious Jews would not be a likely suspect, as they held tight to their Jewish roots and Hebrew language if possible. It is likely the text was written between 100 BCE and 100 CE. Other than stating that the writer was fluent in Greek and was a Jew concerned with keeping the law, conveying the evils of idolatry, and explaining the necessity of keeping the Jewish bloodline pure.

Even though one scholar contends the text is not Jewish because it does not mention Jewish dietary restrictions, it could be strongly argued that references within the text to Joseph having a table set for him separately from the Egyptians could relate to special dietary customs and rituals.

Most of the confusion regarding the story of Joseph and Aseneth may be cleared up if we assume the two stories contained within the texts are written at different times by different authors. The main observations against the assumption of a single author are the obvious dissimilarities between writing styles and the internal rhythm of the two stories. The first story is a tale of romance with lengthy prayers, metaphors, and symbols of religion. The first story centers on Aseneth's relationship with Joseph and her conversion to Judaism. The plot of the second story revolves around war and military motifs. The second story focuses on Joseph's brothers and the attempt of Pharaoh's son to harm Joseph and to abduct Aseneth so that the son of Pharaoh could marry her. In the second story Joseph is no longer central. Levi becomes the chief protagonist alongside Aseneth.

In the first story symbols abound and images such as the "city of refuge," or the honeycomb and bees are placed in a simplistic and prosaic narrative. The first plot stands on its own, culminating in the marriage of Joseph and Aseneth and the birth of their sons. Since the second plot is built upon the first it could be a later addition, written closer to the second date speculated upon, around the fourth of fifth centuries CE. This timeframe could also explain a Christian influence some scholars believe to be part of the text.

By dividing the text into its two divergent component stories and assuming the first story is a Jewish text written between the first century BCE and the first century CE for the purpose of clarifying the Genesis account, and the second story being a later addition containing possible Christian influences, all questions and various opinions are answered in a single, unified theory regarding the full text.

Recently, a small group of scholars have put forth the idea that the story of Joseph and Aseneth is not really about those characters at all. Instead of counting the text as midrash or an expansion of Genesis, they contend the story was written as a allegory revealing the hidden or lost life of Jesus, his marriage, and the fact that he fathered children. This would be impossible if the texts were written before 20-30 CE. Since the date of the first part of the text is set around 100 BCE – 100 CE there is a greater chance the text was already in circulation when Jesus had reached the age of maturity. If the later dates are assumed it would also cast doubt on the validity of the text since the text could not be considered to be an accurate account of the life of Jesus if the allegory were written four-hundred years after the fact.

There are obvious cautions regarding placing any text into the niche of an allegory without knowing the author's purpose for writing. Once labeled as such, anyone can attempt to stamp an agenda or meaning on a text and explain it away with contrived reasoning. Sometimes a story is simply a story about what is seems to be written about. If one evokes Occam's Razor to cut through the recent frenzy of speculation over the marital state of Jesus, when vision clears and the text is examined outside of buzz of popular controversy one can see no direct evidence of allegorical intent.

If the bride of Jesus were Mary Magdalene, as most who believe in such a theory speculate, there would have been no need of a cleansing and conversion to make her a "spiritual Jew" as in one of the main scenes depicts, if she were already Jewish. If she were not Jewish, Mary the Magdalene would have been a Syro-Phoenician who worshipped the goddess Artemis, not Atum-Ra, as in the story. Artemis was the goddess of the hunt, forests and hills, the moon, and of archery. Her shrine and temple were located in Magdala, a city in Galilee. Jacobovici and Wilson, the two main proponents of the Joseph – Aseneth to Jesus – Mary allegory claim Mary of Magdala was a priestess in the cult of Artemis. There is no evidence to substantiate the claim. They then extend the connection by claiming that since the father of Aseneth was the priest of Ra, Aseneth must be a priestess of Ra.

Jacobovici and Wilson select, seemingly at random, certain parts of the story line of Joseph and Aseneth in an attempt to draw parallels to the story of Mary Magdalene. In one such excursion they point out that seven demons were cast out of Mary and they equate this to the seven virgins attending to Aseneth, since they were, by extension, co-priestesses of Ra through their association to Aseneth, who was a priestess via her association with her father. The thread becomes more and more thin as conjectures pile upon conjecture. There is no evidence the virgins were anything but attendants, serving Aseneth. And even though she was spoiled and privileged, Aseneth still cared for them as sisters. In the biblical story, seven demons were cast out of a woman. In the account of Joseph and Aseneth the virgins simply hear Aseneth mourning and return to their quarters, leaving her to grieve.

After the spiritual conversion of Aseneth in a scene containing a messenger, bees and a honeycomb, Aseneth asks the man from heaven if he would also bless her seven virgins, since she loved them as sisters. He agrees and she calls he attendants to her side. The man prays for them: "May the Lord God Most High bless you. You will be the seven pillars in the City of Refuge and all the daughters of the house of the Village of Refuge who choose shall enter and upon you they shall rest forever."

Nowhere in any texts, ancient or new, does one find a man or messenger of God blessing demons.

The seven virgins, according to Jacobovici and Wilson allegory theory, become pillars of the church, but one of the only times seven powerful women of the Christian faith are mentioned as a group is in a Gnostic text called, The First Apocalypse of James, 40:25-26. The manuscript was written around the end of the second century C.E. and is from the Valentinian branch of Gnosticism. In this little text James asks Jesus: 'who are the seven women who have been your disciples?' Only four women are named outright: 'Salome, Mariam, Martha and Arsinoe'. Many believe the seven would have included Mary Magdalene, but since she is never mentioned there is no direct proof. This would have made Mary part of the group and not the leader of it as Aseneth was the governess or leader of her virgins. There is no support for the idea that Aseneth's seven virgins represent the seven demons that possessed Mary Magdalene.

Further, the picture of Jesus as a poor rabbi with no place to lay his head, as painted by the gospels, flies in the face of the rich and powerful Joseph, who Aseneth first glimpses as he drives up in a chariot with a golden awning, wearing the finest of robes. This picture of Jesus is best representative of his place in heaven after his death and resurrection, and not as one having been rejected and crucified in his earthly existence. Any connection or allegory between the Jewish text of Joseph and Aseneth and the Gnostic Christian idea of the marriage between Jesus of Nazareth and Mary the Magdalene seems to be in the best interest of controversy and profit, and not history or investigative process. The theory of allegory between Joseph and Jesus or between Aseneth and Mary should be dismissed.

We shall treat the story of Joseph and Aseneth as an expansion of Genesis, written in a midrash style in order to explain and clarify the actions of the pious Jew, Joseph, in his divinely guided ascent from betrayal and prison to the place of as a leader in Egypt, set there by God to help save his people from a coming famine.

The book is placed, by most scholars, in the category of the pseudepigrapha. Pseudepigrapha are works or texts whose authorship is falsely attributed it to a figure (usually famous) of the past. The Book of Enoch would be such a work.

Pseudepigraphy covers the false ascription of names of authors to works, even to authentic works that make no such claim within their text. Thus a widely accepted but an incorrect attribution of authorship may make a completely authentic text pseudepigraphical. In Old Testament biblical studies, the term Pseudepigrapha typically refers to an assorted collection of Jewish religious writings penned between 300 BCE and 300 CE, although these dates tend to be a bit fluid. They are distinguished by Protestants from the Deuterocanonical (Catholic and Orthodox) or Apocrypha (Protestant), the books that appear in the Septuagint and Vulgate but not in the Hebrew Bible or in Protestant Bibles.

The text of Joseph and Aseneth never reveals its author or narrator but this is a wide category, including books of assumed or accepted authorship. Thus, it does pass the primary requirement to be categorized as pseudepigraphical.

We shall view the first part of the book as the first and primary text, written between 100 BCE and 100 CE, with a higher probability of the date being closer to 100 BCE since it was in that range that the midrash type of narrative was more common. The second part of the story we shall view as a sequel to the first and written later, probably around 400CE. It is the continuation of the first story added to tie together statements in part one regarding Aseneth being desired by the son of Pharaoh. It was also added to teach a moral lesson of forgiveness and "turning the other cheek." Some scholars believe this concept of "non-retribution" for harmful acts done by others is a Christian concept, which would place the second part of the story in the arena of Christian literature, and not Jewish writings. This could be true, but most major religions hold this seed of truth within its teaching.

An example of such early teaching is **The Dhammapada,** written by Buddha around 500 BCE.

Chapter I - The Twin Verses
1. All that we are is the result of what we have thought: it is founded on our thoughts, it is made up of our thoughts. If a man speaks or acts with an evil thought, pain follows him, as the wheel follows the foot of the ox that draws the carriage.

2. All that we are is the result of what we have thought: it is founded on our thoughts, it is made up of our thoughts. If a man speaks or acts with a pure thought, happiness follows him, like a shadow that never leaves him.

3. "He abused me, he beat me, he defeated me, he robbed me," – in those who harbor such thoughts hatred will never cease.

4. "He abused me, he beat me, he defeated me, he robbed me," – in those who do not harbor such thoughts hatred will cease.

5. For hatred does not cease by hatred at any time: hatred ceases by love, this is an old rule.

6. The world does not know that we must all come to an end here; – but those who know it, their quarrels cease at once.

(Feasting at Wisdom's Table, published by Fifth Estate Publishing)

Even though these verses proclaim the concepts of forgiveness and non-retribution, we certainly do not believe the book of Joseph and Aseneth was a Buddhist text. Likewise, we do not have to label the text as Christian simply because it teaches these principles. Although the second part of the text of Joseph and Aseneth was likely written around 400 CE and could have Christian influences, the story does not have pro-Christian rhetoric, conversion stories, or any attempt to evangelize. The most that could be said is that there may have been some cross-cultural influences. Even this statement seems to indicate that some scholars do not believe Judaism was openly teaching forgiveness or a sense of moral strength given to non-retribution at the time of the writing of the second part of the book. This view would be incorrect.

Indeed, the biblical version of Joseph shows no compunction or hesitation toward forgiveness, as Joseph welcomed, sheltered, and fed the brothers who had in the past been so cruel to him. All was forgiven. The events of taunting and bullying, the horrible act of throwing him into a pit, the mercilessness it took to sell him into slavery, all was forgiven. Evil was repaid with caring. Thus, the story itself proves wrong the scholars that would hint that the kind of moral stance of forgiveness was not taught in the Torah.

Genesis 42 Holman Christian Standard Bible (HCSB)
Joseph's Brothers in Egypt
42 When Jacob learned that there was grain in Egypt, he said to his sons, "Why do you keep looking at each other? 2 Listen," he went on, "I have heard there is grain in Egypt. Go down there and buy some for us so that we will live and not die." 3 So 10 of Joseph's brothers went down to buy grain from Egypt. 4 But Jacob did not send Joseph's brother Benjamin with his brothers, for he thought, "Something might happen to him."
5 The sons of Israel were among those who came to buy grain, for the famine was in the land of Canaan. 6 Joseph was in charge of the

country; he sold grain to all its people. His brothers came and bowed down before him with their faces to the ground. 7 When Joseph saw his brothers, he recognized them, but he treated them like strangers and spoke harshly to them.

"Where do you come from?" he asked.

"From the land of Canaan to buy food," they replied.

8 Although Joseph recognized his brothers, they did not recognize him. 9 Joseph remembered his dreams about them and said to them, "You are spies. You have come to see the weakness[a] of the land."

10 "No, my lord. Your servants have come to buy food," they said.

11 "We are all sons of one man. We are honest; your servants are not spies."

12 "No," he said to them. "You have come to see the weakness of the land."

13 But they replied, "We, your servants, were 12 brothers, the sons of one man in the land of Canaan. The youngest is now[b] with our father, and one is no longer living."

14 Then Joseph said to them, "I have spoken:[c] 'You are spies!' 15 This is how you will be tested: As surely as Pharaoh lives, you will not leave this place unless your youngest brother comes here. 16 Send one from among you to get your brother. The rest of you will be imprisoned so that your words can be tested to see if they are true. If they are not, then as surely as Pharaoh lives, you are spies!" 17 So Joseph imprisoned them together for three days.

18 On the third day Joseph said to them, "I fear God – do this and you will live. 19 If you are honest, let one of you[d] be confined to the guardhouse, while the rest of you go and take grain to relieve the hunger of your households. 20 Bring your youngest brother to me so that your words can be confirmed; then you won't die." And they consented to this.

21 Then they said to each other, "Obviously, we are being punished for what we did to our brother. We saw his deep distress when he pleaded with us, but we would not listen. That is why this trouble has come to us."

22 But Reuben replied: "Didn't I tell you not to harm the boy? But you wouldn't listen. Now we must account for his blood!"[e]

23 They did not realize that Joseph understood them, since there was an interpreter between them. 24 He turned away from them and wept. Then he turned back and spoke to them. He took Simeon from them and had him bound before their eyes. 25 Joseph then gave orders to fill their containers with grain, return each man's money to his sack, and give them provisions for their journey. This order was carried out. 26 They loaded the grain on their donkeys and left there.

The Brothers Return Home

27 At the place where they lodged for the night, one of them opened his sack to get feed for his donkey, and he saw his money there at the top of the bag. 28 He said to his brothers, "My money has been returned! It's here in my bag." Their hearts sank. Trembling, they

turned to one another and said, "What is this that God has done to us?"

29 When they reached their father Jacob in the land of Canaan, they told him all that had happened to them: 30 "The man who is the lord of the country spoke harshly to us and accused us of spying on the country. 31 But we told him: We are honest and not spies. 32 We were 12 brothers, sons of the same[f] father. One is no longer living, and the youngest is now[g] with our father in the land of Canaan. 33 The man who is the lord of the country said to us, 'This is how I will know if you are honest: Leave one brother with me, take food to relieve the hunger of your households, and go. 34 Bring back your youngest brother to me, and I will know that you are not spies but honest men. I will then give your brother back to you, and you can trade in the country.'"

35 As they began emptying their sacks, there in each man's sack was his bag of money! When they and their father saw their bags of money, they were afraid.

36 Their father Jacob said to them, "You have deprived me of my sons. Joseph is gone and Simeon is gone. Now you want to take Benjamin. Everything happens to me!"

37 Then Reuben said to his father, "You can kill my two sons if I don't bring him back to you. Put him in my care,[h] and I will return him to you."

38 But Jacob answered, "My son will not go down with you, for his brother is dead and he alone is left. If anything happens to him on your journey, you will bring my gray hairs down to Sheol in sorrow."

Footnotes:

Genesis 42:9 Lit nakedness

Genesis 42:13 Or today

Genesis 42:14 Lit "That which I spoke to you saying

Genesis 42:19 Lit your brothers

Genesis 42:22 Lit Even his blood is being sought

Genesis 42:32 Lit of our

Genesis 42:32 Or today

Genesis 42:37 Lit hand

Genesis 43 Holman Christian Standard Bible (HCSB)

Decision to Return to Egypt

43 Now the famine in the land was severe. 2 When they had used up the grain they had brought back from Egypt, their father said to them, "Go back and buy us some food."

3 But Judah said to him, "The man specifically warned us: 'You will not see me again unless your brother is with you.' 4 If you will send our brother with us, we will go down and buy food for you. 5 But if you will not send him, we will not go, for the man said to us, 'You will not see me again unless your brother is with you.'"

6 *"Why did you cause me so much trouble?"* Israel asked. *"Why did you tell the man that you had another brother?"*

7 They answered, *"The man kept asking about us and our family: 'Is your father still alive? Do you have another brother?' And we answered him accordingly. How could we know that he would say, 'Bring your brother here'?"*

8 Then Judah said to his father Israel, *"Send the boy with me. We will be on our way so that we may live and not die — neither we, nor you, nor our children. 9 I will be responsible for him. You can hold me personally accountable![a] If I do not bring him back to you and set him before you, I will be guilty before you forever. 10 If we had not wasted time, we could have come back twice by now."*

11 Then their father Israel said to them, *"If it must be so, then do this: Put some of the best products of the land in your packs and take them down to the man as a gift — some balsam and some honey, aromatic gum and resin, pistachios and almonds. 12 Take twice as much money with you. Return the money that was returned to you in the top of your bags. Perhaps it was a mistake. 13 Take your brother also, and go back at once to the man. 14 May God Almighty cause the man to be merciful to you so that he will release your other brother and Benjamin to you. As for me, if I am deprived of my sons, then I am deprived."*

The Return to Egypt

15 *The men took this gift, double the amount of money, and Benjamin. They made their way down to Egypt and stood before Joseph.*

16 *When Joseph saw Benjamin with them, he said to his steward,[b] "Take the men to my house. Slaughter an animal and prepare it, for they will eat with me at noon." 17 The man did as Joseph had said and brought them to Joseph's house.*

18 *But the men were afraid because they were taken to Joseph's house. They said, "We have been brought here because of the money that was returned in our bags the first time. They intend to overpower us, seize us, make us slaves, and take our donkeys." 19 So they approached Joseph's steward[c] and spoke to him at the doorway of the house.*

20 *They said, "Sir, we really did come down here the first time only to buy food. 21 When we came to the place where we lodged for the night and opened our bags of grain, each one's money was at the top of his bag! It was the full amount of our money, and we have brought it back with us. 22 We have brought additional money with us to buy food. We don't know who put our money in the bags."*

23 *Then the steward said, "May you be well. Don't be afraid. Your God and the God of your father must have put treasure in your bags. I received your money." Then he brought Simeon out to them. 24 The steward brought the men into Joseph's house, gave them water to wash their feet, and got feed for their donkeys. 25 Since the men had heard that they were going to eat a meal there, they prepared*

their gift for Joseph's arrival at noon. 26 When Joseph came home, they brought him the gift they had carried into the house, and they bowed to the ground before him.

27 He asked if they were well, and he said, "How is your elderly father that you told me about? Is he still alive?"

28 They answered, "Your servant our father is well. He is still alive." And they bowed down to honor him.

29 When he looked up and saw his brother Benjamin, his mother's son, he asked, "Is this your youngest brother that you told me about?" Then he said, "May God be gracious to you, my son." 30 Joseph hurried out because he was overcome with emotion for his brother, and he was about to weep. He went into an inner room to weep. 31 Then he washed his face and came out. Regaining his composure, he said, "Serve the meal."

32 They served him by himself, his brothers by themselves, and the Egyptians who were eating with him by themselves, because Egyptians could not eat with Hebrews, since that is abhorrent to them. 33 They were seated before him in order by age, from the firstborn to the youngest. The men looked at each other in astonishment. 34 Portions were served to them from Joseph's table, and Benjamin's portion was five times larger than any of theirs. They drank, and they got intoxicated with Joseph.

Footnotes:

Genesis 43:9 Lit can seek him from my hand

Genesis 43:16 Lit to the one who was over his house

Genesis 43:19 Lit approached the one who was over the house

Joseph's Final Test

44 Then Joseph commanded his steward: "Fill the men's bags with as much food as they can carry, and put each one's money at the top of his bag. 2 Put my cup, the silver one, at the top of the youngest one's bag, along with his grain money." So he did as Joseph told him.

3 At morning light, the men were sent off with their donkeys. 4 They had not gone very far from the city when Joseph said to his steward, "Get up. Pursue the men, and when you overtake them, say to them, 'Why have you repaid evil for good?[a] 5 Isn't this the cup that my master drinks from and uses for divination? What you have done is wrong!'"

6 When he overtook them, he said these words to them. 7 They said to him, "Why does my lord say these things? Your servants could not possibly do such a thing. 8 We even brought back to you from the land of Canaan the money we found at the top of our bags. How could we steal gold and silver from your master's house? 9 If any of us is[b] found to have it, he must die, and we also will become my lord's slaves."

10 The steward replied, "What you have said is right, but only the one who is found to have it will be my slave, and the rest of you will be blameless."

11 *So each one quickly lowered his sack to the ground and opened it.*
12 *The steward searched, beginning with the oldest and ending with
the youngest, and the cup was found in Benjamin's sack.* 13 *Then
they tore their clothes, and each one loaded his donkey and returned
to the city.*
14 *When Judah and his brothers reached Joseph's house, he was still
there. They fell to the ground before him.* 15 *"What is this you have
done?" Joseph said to them. "Didn't you know that a man like me
could uncover the truth by divination?"*
16 *"What can we say to my lord?" Judah replied. "How can we
plead? How can we justify ourselves? God has exposed your
servants' iniquity. We are now my lord's slaves — both we and the
one in whose possession the cup was found."*
17 *Then Joseph said, "I swear that I will not do this. The man in
whose possession the cup was found will be my slave. The rest of you
can go in peace to your father."*

Judah's Plea for Benjamin
18 *But Judah approached him and said, "Sir, please let your servant
speak personally to my lord.[c] Do not be angry with your servant,
for you are like Pharaoh.* 19 *My lord asked his servants, 'Do you
have a father or a brother?'* 20 *and we answered my lord, 'We have
an elderly father and a younger brother, the child of his old age. The
boy's brother is dead. He is the only one of his mother's sons left, and
his father loves him.'* 21 *Then you said to your servants, 'Bring him*

to me so that I can see him.' 22 But we said to my lord, 'The boy cannot leave his father. If he were to leave, his father would die.' 23 Then you said to your servants, 'If your younger brother does not come down with you, you will not see me again.'

24 "This is what happened when we went back to your servant my father: We reported your words to him. 25 But our father said, 'Go again, and buy us some food.' 26 We told him, 'We cannot go down unless our younger brother goes with us. So if our younger brother isn't with us, we cannot see the man.' 27 Your servant my father said to us, 'You know that my wife bore me two sons. 28 One left – I said that he must have been torn to pieces – and I have never seen him again. 29 If you also take this one from me and anything happens to him, you will bring my gray hairs down to Sheol in sorrow.'

30 "So if I come to your servant my father and the boy is not with us – his life is wrapped up with the boy's life – 31 when he sees that the boy is not with us, he will die. Then your servants will have brought the gray hairs of your servant our father down to Sheol in sorrow. 32 Your servant became accountable to my father for the boy, saying, 'If I do not return him to you, I will always bear the guilt for sinning against you, my father.' 33 Now please let your servant remain here as my lord's slave, in place of the boy. Let him go back with his brothers. 34 For how can I go back to my father without the boy? I could not bear to see the grief that would overwhelm my father."

Footnotes:

Genesis 44:4 LXX adds Why have you stolen my silver cup?

Genesis 44:9 Lit If your servants are

Genesis 44:18 Lit speak a word in my lord's ears

Genesis 45 Holman Christian Standard Bible (HCSB)

Joseph Reveals His Identity

45 Joseph could no longer keep his composure in front of all his attendants,[a] so he called out, "Send everyone away from me!" No one was with him when he revealed his identity to his brothers. 2 But he wept so loudly that the Egyptians heard it, and also Pharaoh's household heard it. 3 Joseph said to his brothers, "I am Joseph! Is my father still living?" But they could not answer him because they were terrified in his presence.

4 Then Joseph said to his brothers, "Please, come near me," and they came near. "I am Joseph, your brother," he said, "the one you sold into Egypt. 5 And now don't be worried or angry with yourselves for selling me here, because God sent me ahead of you to preserve life. 6 For the famine has been in the land these two years, and there will be five more years without plowing or harvesting. 7 God sent me ahead of you to establish you as a remnant within the land and to keep you alive by a great deliverance.[b] 8 Therefore it was not you who sent me here, but God. He has made me a father to Pharaoh, lord of his entire household, and ruler over all the land of Egypt.

9 *"Return quickly to my father and say to him, 'This is what your son Joseph says: "God has made me lord of all Egypt. Come down to me without delay. 10 You can settle in the land of Goshen and be near me — you, your children, and grandchildren, your sheep, cattle, and all you have. 11 There I will sustain you, for there will be five more years of famine. Otherwise, you, your household, and everything you have will become destitute."' 12 Look! Your eyes and my brother Benjamin's eyes can see that it is I , Joseph, who am[c] speaking to you. 13 Tell my father about all my glory in Egypt and about all you have seen. And bring my father here quickly."*

14 Then Joseph threw his arms around Benjamin and wept, and Benjamin wept on his shoulder. 15 Joseph kissed each of his brothers as he wept,[d] and afterward his brothers talked with him.

The Return for Jacob

16 When the news reached Pharaoh's palace, "Joseph's brothers have come," Pharaoh and his servants were pleased. 17 Pharaoh said to Joseph, "Tell your brothers, 'Do this: Load your animals and go on back to the land of Canaan. 18 Get your father and your families, and come back to me. I will give you the best of the land of Egypt, and you can eat from the richness of the land.' 19 You are also commanded, 'Do this: Take wagons from the land of Egypt for your young children and your wives and bring your father here. 20 Do not be concerned about your belongings, for the best of all the land of Egypt is yours.'"

21 *The sons of Israel did this. Joseph gave them wagons as Pharaoh had commanded, and he gave them provisions for the journey.* 22 *He gave each of the brothers changes of clothes, but he gave Benjamin 300 pieces of silver and five changes of clothes.* 23 *He sent his father the following: 10 donkeys carrying the best products of Egypt and 10 female donkeys carrying grain, food, and provisions for his father on the journey.* 24 *So Joseph sent his brothers on their way, and as they were leaving, he said to them, "Don't argue on the way."*

25 *So they went up from Egypt and came to their father Jacob in the land of Canaan.* 26 *They said, "Joseph is still alive, and he is ruler over all the land of Egypt!" Jacob was stunned,[e] for he did not believe them.* 27 *But when they told Jacob all that Joseph had said to them, and when he saw the wagons that Joseph had sent to transport him, the spirit of their father Jacob revived.*

28 *Then Israel said, "Enough! My son Joseph is still alive. I will go to see him before I die."*

Footnotes:

Genesis 45:1 Lit all those standing about him

Genesis 45:7 Or keep alive for you many survivors

Genesis 45:12 Lit that my mouth is

Genesis 45:15 Lit brothers, and he wept over them

Genesis 45:26 Lit Jacob's heart was numb

The story expands on a few short statements made in the middle of the biblical account of Joseph's extraordinary life. Up to now we have seen the entire biblical account, but now we will look more closely at the lives of Joseph and Aseneth, and how their unlikely courtship, marriage, and personal triumphs produced two sons, Ephraim and Manasseh, who became the half-tribes counted in the lineage of the tribes of Israel.

This translation of Joseph and Aseneth is unique and crafted for the modern reader. It conveys the meaning of the text while avoiding archaic words, confusing sentence structure, and tangled syntax encountered in older translations. The combined body of work from Rivka Nir, David Cook, H.F.D. Sparks, James H. Charlesworth and other great scholars informed this translation. A list of other authors, publishers, fragments and manuscripts accessed in the production of this follows:

Fabricius published a fragment from a Codex Baroccianus in his Codex pseudepigraphns. Vol. H, 85-102 ; but the complete text according to four manuscripts was first published by Batiffol, Studia patristica, etudes d'ancienne littera- ture chretienne, fasc. 1-2, Paris, 1889-1890. pp. 1-87.

The Latin text, which was formerly the main source for the knowledge of the legend, is an extract. It is printed in Vincentius Belloracensis (13th century), SpecuJiun historiale, Vol. 1, lib. n, cap. 118-124, and reprinted in Fabricius, Codex pseudepi- graphns, I, 774-784.

The complete Latin text from which this extract was taken, was discovered by James in two MSS. of English origin (13th-14th century) at Cambridge, and is given in Batiffol's work, fasc. 2, pp. 89-115.- According to Batiftol, the translation.

A Syriac version was published by Laud, in Anecdota Syriaca, III, 1870. pp. 15-46. According to Wright {Catalogue of Syriac MSS. in the British Museum, p. 1047) this text (Add. 17202) belongs to the sixth or seventh century. Batiffol is inclined to ascribe it to the middle of the sixth century

An Armenian translation was published by the Mechitharists of Venice in Revue polyhistore, Vol. XLIII, 1885, pp. 200-206, XLIV, 1888, pp. 25-34."

An Ethiopian version is mentioned at the end of an Ethiopian M.S. belonging to the fifteenth century, as may be seen from A. Dillniann's catalogue of Ethiopian MSS. in the British Museum.

We shall treat the entire text as one penned by a Jewish author for Jewish readers. Having covered the full background and history of the text, along with what some of the better-known scholars have to say about the text of Joseph and Aseneth, let us now examine the book of Joseph and Aseneth itself. The main body of the text of Joseph and Aseneth will be in plain font. Author's notes and other comments will be placed in italicized font within the body of the text to aid in explanation and clarification.

Joseph and Aseneth
Part One

I.   In the second month of the first year in the seven years of plenty, Pharaoh sent Joseph out to go throughout the entire land of Egypt.

(Joseph was inspecting the land and crops in order to prepare for a famine, which he predicted based on the dreams of Pharaoh, which Joseph had interpreted.)

2. On the eighteenth day of the fourth month of the first year Joseph arrived in the district, which contained the city of Heliopolis.

Heliopolis is an ancient city in Egypt that the Greeks had renamed. The name means "City of the Sun" or "City of Helios". Its Arabic name means "Eye of the Sun". Heliopolis was one of the oldest cities of ancient Egypt, the capital of the 13th Lower Egyptian nome (a subnational administrative division). It is now found at the northeast edge of Cairo.

3. The corn in that land was as plentiful as the sands of the sea and Joseph was collecting (all the) corn. 4. In that city there was a man who was the chief of all Pharaoh's governors and administrators. 5. He was very wise and generous, and he was wealthy. The name of Pharaoh's counselor was Petephres, the priest of Heliopolis.

Heliopolis is the city of "On" mentioned in the Hebrew bible. It was renamed Heliopolis by the Greeks in recognition of the fact that the sun god Ra (Helios mean sun in Greek) presided there. Heliopolis has been occupied since the Predynastic Period, with extensive building campaigns during the Old and Middle Kingdoms. Today it is mostly destroyed; its temples and other buildings were used for the construction of medieval Cairo. The only surviving remnant of Heliopolis is the Temple of Re-Atum obelisk located in Al-Masalla in Al-Matariyyah, Cairo. It was erected by Senusret I of the Twelfth dynasty, and still stands in its original position. Petephres was the high priest of the cult of Ra, the sun god, in the time of Joseph.

6. Petephres had a young daughter who was eighteen years old. She was tall, graceful, and beautiful. She was more comely than any other virgin in Egypt. 7. She was very different from the daughters of the Egyptians. However, she was like the daughters of the Hebrews in every way. 8. She

was tall like Sarah, beautiful like Rebecca, and had a shapely body like Rachel. She was a virgin, and her name was Aseneth. 9. Her beauty was famous throughout all that land. Even the most remote parts had heard of Aseneth's beauty. The men, who were the sons of the officials and administrators of the king, sought her hand in marriage. 10. Because of her there was ongoing rivalries and fights between the boys as they fought over Aseneth. 11. The eldest son of Pharaoh heard about Aseneth and begged his father to give him Aseneth as a wife. 12. He said to his father, "Give me Aseneth, the daughter of Petephres the priest and first man (head of the city) of Heliopolis, as my wife." But Pharaoh, his father, said to him, "You should not want a wife of lower station than yourself. 13. You are the king of all the land 14. Do you not understand the daughter of Joakim, the king of Moab is betrothed to you? She is a queen and she is very beautiful. You should take her as your wife."

II. Aseneth was arrogant and proud. She viewed all men with contempt and seemed to hate them all. Her father, Petephres, had a tower in his house, which was large and very high. There he kept his daughter so that neither man nor boy would see her. 2. The top floor of the tower had ten rooms.

It is difficult to know if the father of Aseneth was over-protective to the extent it caused Aseneth to be xenophobic in general or if she did not like men specifically. We are told later that Aseneth wished to keep the way of life she enjoyed in her father's house. Marriage would have changed that, since Aseneth would be forced to live with her husband and be provided for by him, according to his rank and wealth. Her station was high enough there would be few prospective husbands that would equal or elevate her status and standard of living.

3. The first room was spacious and comfortable. The flooring of the room was made of purple stones, and its walls had a facade made of various types of precious stones of many colors and cut flat. 4. There was gold plating on the ceiling. Within that room were countess statues of Egyptian gods, all made of gold and silver.
5. And Aseneth reverenced and worshipped them all, offering sacrifices daily to them.

6. In the second room were chests full of all the gold and silver adornments and treasure needed to dress in fine fashion. 7. Aseneth had garments of fine linen, which were woven with gold and priceless precious stones. 8. There were adornments used to announce her virginity in that room also.

9. The third room contained items of great value from all the of the lands. These rooms were used to house the riches of Aseneth.

10. Aseneth had seven virgins attending her and each of her seven attendants had a room of their own. These took up the remaining seven rooms. 11. The virgins were the same age as Aseneth and all the girls were beautiful and were all born on the same night as Aseneth. They were like the stars in the sky, and no man or boy ever touched or saw them.

12. It was in the large room with three large windows that Aseneth spent most of her time and where her virginity was nurtured (protected).

It is obvious that virginity was extremely important at the time of the writing of "Joseph and Aseneth." In the Jewish viewpoint, every marriage was expected to produce offspring since neither society nor the family could survive long without helpers and those to inherit land and money to carry on the family name. Marriage without sex was considered a curse to the ancients. It made sense that Hebrew law required the marriage to be consummated before it had any legal effect. Thus, it was sex that made the relationship a marriage. Grooms insisted their brides be a virgin and be able to prove it. If the groom believed he had received a bride who was not a virgin he had the right to challenge her family to produce the proof. If the sheets from the marital bed did not show the required blood then the men of the village would stone her to death in front of her father's house, where she had lived. If the elders were satisfied that the bride had been a virgin then the groom would be whipped and required to pay 100 shekels of silver to her father. The husband would lose the right to divorce her, ever. (Deuteronomy 22: 13-21)

Try, as men may to guard their bloodline, cuckoldry was always possible. Today in the U.S. estimates run between 5 – 10%. That is to say that between 5 to 10 out of every 100 men are raising another man's child unknowingly. In ancient times, the simple suggestion was such an insult it could result in fights to the death. Virginity and certainty of paternity were the pipelines through which inheritance, land, wealth and status flowed.

13. From one window she could see the courtyard to the east. From the second window she watched the activity in the street to the north, and the third window opened to the south. 14. Facing the east was her bed, made of gold. 15. The coverlet on her bed was made of purple linen woven with golden threads and embroidered with blue. 16 Aseneth always slept alone. No man or woman ever even sat upon the bed. Only Aseneth ever sat on it. 17. There was a large courtyard encompassing the house, with a high wall constructed of large square stones. 18. The courtyard had four gates of entry, which were overlaid

with iron. Eighteen young men, armed and strong, guarded the gates.

19. The walls were lined inside the courtyard with every kind of beautiful fruiting tree. Now was harvest time and all the fruit from the trees were ripe and ready to pick. 20. On the right side of the courtyard was a rich (lively) spring, which flowed into a huge cistern made of marble, situated just below the spring. The cistern gathered water from the spring. The water overflowed into a river running through the midst of the courtyard. The flowing river watered all the trees.

III. Joseph drew near the city of Heliopolis. 2. Joseph was lord over his men and so as he approached the city, he sent twelve men in to town before him to speak to Petephres, the priest of Heliopolis. 3. Joseph's message said, "The time draws near noon and the sun's heat is overpowering. We need to stop for a mid-day meal. I would enjoy some refreshment under your roof. May I be your guest today?

4. When Petephres heard this, he was overjoyed and said, 5. "Blessed be the Lord, the God of Joseph."

The utterance, "Blessed be the Lord, the God of Joseph" seems very strange coming from the lips of the High Priest of the Sun God. It could be a twist on the story to tell the reader that even pagans respected the Jewish God. However, it could simply speak to the flexibility of polytheistic societies to easily incorporate another god into their pantheon.

And Petephres called his servant who was over the house and said to him, 6. "Hurry. Get my house in order, and prepare a great feast. Joseph, the mighty man of God, is visiting today." 7. Aseneth heard that her father and mother had come back from the field of their inherited family estate in the country. 8. She was very happy and said to herself, "My father and my mother have come back from the family estate in the country so I will go see them. 9. And Aseneth rushed into the room where her robes were laid out and put on one that was made of fine blue linen, which was woven with gold. Then she placed a golden belt round her waist. She put bracelets round her wrists and ankles. She on put golden pants and placed a necklace round her neck. 10. All the bracelets she wore were made of precious stones with the names of Egyptian gods and idols inscribed and stamped on them. 11. She topped off her wardrobe by placing a tiara on her head and tied a jeweled headband round her temples. Then she covered her head with a veil.

Tiara and crown, diadem and headband symbolizing authority and
sovereignty are terms used in this passage.

IV. And she hurried and descended the staircase from her
place on the top floor, greeting her mother and father as she
came. 2. Petephres and his wife were overjoyed to see their
daughter Aseneth adorned as the bride of God.

"Bride of God" is an odd phrase. On first impression it carries with
it a Christian tone, since the church is referred to as the bride of
Christ. But the sun god also had a wife. The title of God's Wife, Wife
of Amun or Wife of Ra first appeared during the Tenth and Twelfth
dynasties, when non-royal women, among those serving the sun god
as priestesses, held the title and position. The office of the God's Wife
reached the height of its political power during the late Third
Intermediate Period of Egypt when Shepenupet I, Osorkon III's
daughter, was first appointed to the position at Thebes. The office
continued until 525 BCE under Nitocris' successor,
Ankhnesneferibre, when the Persians overthrew Egypt's last Saite
ruler, Psamtik III (526–525 BCE), and enslaved his daughter.
Thereafter, the office of God's Wife disappears from history.

It should be noted that the sun gods Amun and Ra merged. Amun
was one of the eight ancient Egyptian gods who formed the Ogdoad

of Hermopolis. He was the god of the air. However, during the Twelfth dynasty (Middle Kingdom) Amun was adopted in Thebes as the King of the gods with Mut as his consort. Ahmose I, the first Pharaoh of the New Kingdom believed that Amun had helped him drive the Hyksos from Egypt. He was also adopted into the Ennead of Heliopolis when he merged with the ancient sun god, Ra, to become Amun-Ra.

There is debate as to whether the Hyksos, the foreigners that took over Egypt, were actually the Jews. One theory explains that as the Jews began to multiply to a dangerous population the Pharaoh became nervous, seeing that the Hyksos had the wherewithal to depose him. Their population was great and they were strong people. Since they had not assimilated into Egyptian culture and did not regard the Pharaoh as divine, they could attack and try to make Egypt into their country with their culture. This scenario may have actually occurred. Around the year 1700 BCE the Hyksos invaded. They successfully took over Egypt and a succession of six kings took power, known as "the Great Hyksos Pharaohs."

Josephus Flavius, Jewish historian of the 1st century CE and author of The Antiquities of the Jews, identified the Hyksos with the Hebrews. Most historians today disagree, but there are some who hold to this theory due to the striking similarities between the Hyksos and the Jews. The Hyksos were from an alien culture and did *not follow the Egyptian religion. The Hyksos Pharaohs never claimed to be gods, nor did they build for themselves any monuments. They moved the capital of Egypt to the land of Goshen, which is the area the Jews settled.*

The Medrash tells us that Moses was a king in the Sudan for a long period of time, and we do have evidence that the Hyksos people ruled not only in Egypt, but also in the Sudan and Libya. However, evidence shows that the Jews kept a low profile in Egypt. They had little to do with the government but they played a large part in the economy of Egypt.

In about 1560 BCE, the local, indigenous population expelled the Hyksos in a rebellion. This marked the beginning of the New Empire and a radical change in Egyptian society. Egypt became xenophobic, killing or enslaving foreigners. This shift corresponds with the period of Jewish enslavement in Egypt. The Jews would gain their freedom once again in the time of Moses. Their escape would be documented in the book of Exodus.

Petephres and his wife unpacked all the goods they had brought back from the fields of their inheritance and gave them to their daughter. 4. Aseneth was ecstatic when she saw all the good things. There were fruits such as grapes, pomegranates, figs and the dates, and they were all ripe and delightful. There were beautiful doves as well. 5. Then Petephres said to his daughter Aseneth, "My child": she said, "Yes, sir." 6. And he said to her, "Please sit down between your mother and I. I want to speak to you about what is on my mind." So, Aseneth sat down between her father and her mother. 7. And her father took her right hand and said to her, "My child..." Aseneth said, "Father, go ahead, speak." 8. And Petephres said to her, "You see, Joseph, the mighty man of God, will be visiting us today. Pharaoh has appointed him as ruler of all the land of Egypt, and that includes our land. He will be in charge of distributing corn throughout the country to save everyone from the coming famine, which will be upon this land."

9. "Joseph worships God. He is a man of good judgment, wisdom, and knowledge and he is a virgin like you are to this day. The grace and spirit of the Lord (his) God is with him. 10. For these reasons I will give you to him as his wife, my child. You will be his bride, and he shall be your husband for ever."

11. But, when Aseneth heard what her father said, she broke out in great beads of sweat all over. She was so angry she was in a rage. She looked askance at her father. 12. She said, "Why, sir, should you speak to me like this. You are my father, but

you talk to me as if I were a prisoner of a different race, like a slave or fugitive to be sold. 13. Isn't this man the Canaanite shepherd's son that was sold by his father? 14. Didn't he have sex with his master's wife, and did his master not throw him into a dark prison where he stayed? Isn't it true that Pharaoh only brought him out of prison because he interpreted his dream? 15. No! I will marry the king's oldest son because he is king of all the land of Egypt." 16. When Petephres heard the way she spoke so angry and arrogantly to him he thought it best to say nothing more to his daughter about Joseph.

Aseneth had the story wrong. She was relying on gossip. She was sassy, and disrespectful to her parents. She was a typical teenager. Her father waited for her to cool off and think about how she was acting.

V. Suddenly one of Petephres's young servant boys burst in and said, 2. " I saw Joseph at the gates of our court." Aseneth quickly left her parents and ran upstairs. She went into her room and stood at the big window looking east, toward the gate so she could see Joseph as he entered her father's house.

3. Petephres and his wife and all his extended family went out to meet Joseph. 4. The Eastern gates were opened, and Joseph

entered, sitting in the Pharaoh's second chariot that he had given to Joseph as a ruler. 5. It was drawn by four horses, white as snow, which were yoked together with a bridle studded with gold and with golden reins. The chariot had a golden awning that covered it. 6. And Joseph was wearing a wonderful glittering white uniform and wrapped around him was a fine purple linen robe. 7. On his head was a crown of gold like a wreath with twelve precious stones in it, and above the stones were twelve golden rays. He held a royal scepter in his right hand. The scepter was topped with a divided olive branch laden with fruit.

Cook uses the term "tunic" for both Joseph's uniform and later for the mourning dress Aseneth wears. These are so dissimilar as to need totally different terms. The tunic Joseph wears is part of a uniform, and so we call it a uniform. It is white, finely woven, close fitting, and comes down to about the thigh area. It is worn with a finely crafted bell as the shirt of a dress uniform. The tunic worn by Aseneth is essentially a sack dress. It is a large sack shaped object with holes for arms and head. It has no sleeves. It is coarsely woven and comes down to the knees. It is belted with a plain rope. The coarseness and plainness of the object calls to mind the abject misery of the mourning process.

8. When Joseph entered the courtyard the gates were shut. 9. And no stranger, neither men nor women, could come in. All strangers were shut out because the gate-keepers had shut the doors. 10. Petephres and his wife came to greet Joseph with all the extended family of Petephres, except for their daughter, Aseneth. And they bowed out of respect to Joseph with their faces to the ground. 11. Then Joseph exited his chariot and stretched out his right hand to them.

Petephres and family show the same respect for Joseph as they would to Pharaoh. Joseph and his chariot are adorned in a combination of Egyptian and possible Jewish symbols. Gold and symbols of sun rays abound. Purple is the color of royalty and only nobles could wear the color. The twelve precious stones could call to mind the Urim and Thummim, a breastplate with twelve precious stones embedded in it. The first reference to Urim and Thummim in the Bible is the description in the Book of Exodus concerning the high priest's vestments; the chronologically earliest passage mentioning them, according to textual scholars, is in the Book of Hosea, where it is implied, by reference to the Ephod, that the Urim and Thummim were fundamental elements in the popular form of the Israelite religion, in the mid 8th century BC.
Exodus 28: 15"Fashion a breast piece for making decisions – the work of skilled hands. Make it like the ephod: of gold, and of blue, purple and scarlet yarn, and of finely twisted linen. 16 It is to be

square – a span long and a span wide – and folded double. 17 Four rows of precious stones were mounted on it. The first row shall be carnelian, chrysolite and beryl; 18 the second row shall be turquoise, lapis lazuli and emerald; 19 the third row shall be jacinth, agate and amethyst; 20 the fourth row shall be topaz, onyx and jasper. Mount them in gold filigree settings. 21 There are to be twelve stones, one for each of the names of the sons of Israel, each engraved like a seal with the name of one of the twelve tribes.

VI. Then Aseneth saw Joseph and her soul was pricked and she felt her heart break. Her knees went weak, and she trembled all over. 2. Then she cried out in fear and said, "Where can I go, and where can I hide from him? What will Joseph, the son of God, think of me, because I have spoken badly of him? 3. Where can I run to and where can I hide? There is such a bright light in him so he sees everything. No secret is safe from him. 4. I pray the God of Joseph to have mercy on me because I spoke evil things in ignorance. 5. I am a hopeless wretch because I said, Joseph, the Canaanites' shepherd's son is coming, but now I see the sun from heaven has come to us in his chariot and has entered our house today. 6. I was a reckless fool to hate him and to speak evil of him. I did not realize Joseph is the son of God. 7 What man could ever father such a beautiful person, and what mother's womb could bear such a light? I am a foolish wretch for speaking so badly to my father. 8. Now I will allow my father to give me to Joseph as a domestic servant or a slave, and I will serve him for ever."

VII. When Joseph entered Petephres's house he sat down on a cushion. Phetephres washed his feet and then he had a table placed in front of him, separate from the others because Joseph would not eat with the Egyptians. They were an unclean (unholy/abomination) to Joseph.

2. And Joseph spoke to Petephres and all his relations, saying, "Who is that woman standing in the top floor sun room by the window? Tell her to leave the house." 3. This was because Joseph was afraid she too might attempt to seduce him as had the wives and daughters of the officials and rulers of all the land of Egypt use to attempt to seduce him to have sex with them. 4. And many of the Egyptian wives and daughters had great pains of passion after seeing Joseph because he was very handsome. They would send their messengers to him with numerous gifts as well as amounts of gold and silver. 5. But Joseph always rejected them and sent them back with insults and threats if they did not leave him alone. He would say, "I will not sin before the God of Israel." 6. And Joseph

remembered the face of his father Jacob and his commandments and Joseph kept these in his mind always. Jacob would tell Joseph and his brothers, "Children, be on guard against the foreign woman. Have nothing to do with her. She will be your ruin and destruction. 7. That is the reason Joseph told them, "Tell that woman to leave this house." 8. But Petephres said, "Sir, the woman you have seen on the top floor is not a stranger. She is our daughter. Our daughter is a virgin who rejects men. No strangers have ever seen her, besides you today. 9. We would like for her to come and speak to you if you wish, because our daughter is like you, like your sister." 10. Joseph was delighted because Petephres said, "She is a virgin who rejects men." 11. Then Joseph said to Petephres and his wife, "If she is your daughter, allow her to come. She is like my sister and I will love her like a sister from today on."

VIII. Then Aseneth's mother climbed the stairs to the top floor and brought Aseneth down to meet Joseph. Petephres said to his daughter Aseneth, "Say hello to your brother. He is a virgin just as you are, and he rejects all foreign women just as you reject foreign men." 2. Aseneth said to Joseph, "Joy and blessings to you from God Most High." Joseph responded to her, saying, "May the God who gave life to all things bless you." 3. And Petephres said to Aseneth, "Come closer and kiss your brother." 4. But when she came closer to kiss Joseph, he put out his right hand on her chest between her breasts to stop her.

5. He said, "It is improper for a man who worships God with his mouth and praises the living God, and eats the blesses bread of life, and drinks the blessed cup of everlasting life, and who is anointed with the blessed oil of immortality, to kiss a foreign woman. Your mouth has praised dead and silent idols. Your mouth eats the bread at the table of shame and you strangle on it. Your mouth drinks from their libations and you are ambushed with their cup of treachery. You are anointed with the oil of destruction.

6. A man who worships God will kiss his mother and sister who are from his own tribe and family. With his wife he shares his bed, and together their mouths bless the living God. 7. Likewise, it is not right for a woman who worships God to kiss a foreign man. The act is an abomination in the eyes of God."

Joseph rejects and distains foreign (strange) women, believing them to be unclean. Indeed, he rejects all non-Jews, seeing them as "abominations." To the modern eye, he is racist, showing far less grace and acceptance for the Egyptians than they have for him. To the ancient Jewish reader, Joseph's actions are those of a righteous and pious man who wants nothing more than to be allowed to live a traditionally Jewish way of life, even if he is surrounded by temptations to do otherwise.

Aseneth rejects men and is doubly resistant to foreign men. From the earliest times, people of every tribe, nation, religions, or race have always believed themselves to be superior to those of other tribes, nations, religions, or races. Feelings of superiority are related to xenophobia. These two people, Joseph and Aseneth, are of differing nations and races. Each begins with the viewpoint that they are superior. In the story, Joseph firmly believes that he, as a Jew, is superior. He is also certain the Jews are God's chosen people. They are superior, in part, because they are divinely chosen. In race and religion, Joseph believes he stands above all others in Egypt.

Men often hate each other because they fear each other; they fear each other because they don't know each other; they don't know each other because they cannot communicate; they cannot communicate because they are separated. Dr. Martin Luther King Jr.

8. And when Aseneth heard Joseph's words, she was upset and wept out loud. She could only stare at Joseph as her eyes were filled with tears. 9. And Joseph saw her and his heart was touched by her because he was tender-hearted and

compassionate and reverenced the Lord. He was moved and so he raised his right hand above her head and said,

10. "O Lord God, Most High and Mighty; God of my father Israel,

you gave life to all things and called them from darkness into light.

and from error into truth, and from death into life.

I pray that you give your life and blessing to this virgin.

11. Renew her by your Holy Spirit and remake her by your secret hand. Animate her with your life. Feed her your bread of life.

Let her drink from your cup of blessing.

Count her among your people whom you chose before all things were created.

Allow her to enter into your rest, which you prepared for your chosen people so that we all may live with you in everlasting life."

IX. Aseneth was overflowing with joy at Joseph's blessing, and she departed in haste to her room on the top floor and fell on her bed exhausted. She was happy, but confused and afraid. Sweat poured out of her she and was soaked from the moment she heard what Joseph said to her, which he did in the name of the Most High God. 2. And she wept from the bottom of her heart, and she turned away from the gods she worshiped. Then she decided to wait for evening. 3. At that time Joseph had eaten and drank. He said to his servants, "Hitch the horses to the chariot. I must leave and go through the entire city and then the land. 4. But Petephres asked Joseph to stay the night with them and leave the next day to go on his mission. 5. But Joseph was firm. He said, "No! I must leave now. This is the day God begins his works. But, in eight days time I will return and stay the night here with you."

X. Petephres departed with his relations to their family estate. 2. And Aseneth was left alone with her virgins. Aseneth was depressed, lethargic and she wept until sunset. She ate no bread and drank no water and while all the others slept she was alone and awake. 3. She opened the door and went down to the main door entering the house where and she found the woman who was the doorkeeper asleep with her children.

4. Hurriedly, Aseneth removed the leather curtain covering the door and filled it with ashes. She carried it up to the top floor and spread it out on the floor. 5. And she locked the door and barred it with an iron bar, placing it on the side of the door.

6. Aseneth began to groan (mourning) loudly and weep. The virgin she loved the most heard her mistress groaning, and she woke the other virgins. They hurried in and found the door shut.

We assume the most loved virgins were placed closer to the room of their mistress, much like a seating arrangement at the table of an event where the most important guest are placed closer to the host or head of the table.

7. And she stood listening to Aseneth groaning and weeping and the virgin said, "My lady, why are you so deeply sad? What troubles you? 8. Open the door so we can come in and see you." But Aseneth remained locked in. She spoke to them from inside. "I have a very bad headache. I am on my bed and I feel too weak to get up. I do not have enough strength in my legs to get up to open the door for you right now. Go back to your rooms."

9. Then, Aseneth got up quietly and opened her door stealthily. She went into her second room where she kept her valuables in a chest and her clothing and accessories used to adorn herself. She opened her wardrobe and removed a tunic, dark and black in color.

10. When her youngest brother died she wore this tunic while she was in mourning. Aseneth took off her royal robe and put on the black tunic. She untied her golden belt and tied a rope around her waist. She removed her crown and string of beads from her head. She removed the bracelets from her wrists. 12. Then she took her best robe, which she had removed, and she threw it out of the window for the poor to receive. 13. She gathered her vast number of gold and silver idols and she broke them into small pieces, which she gave out from her window to the poor and needy.

14. And Aseneth gathered together her dinner, which was prepared for royalty and consisted of various fattened animals, as well as fish and meat from a heifer (cow). She took the meals, which were offerings presented to her gods, along with the bottles of wine used for libation offering to her gods. She hurled them all out of the window so dogs would consume them.

15. Then she took the ashes and poured them onto the floor. 16. She wrapped sackcloth around her waist. She removed the hair band she wore to tie her hair back. Then she fell down into the ashes.

17. She beat her breast with her own hands and she wept aloud and lamented all night long. 18. Aseneth stood up from the ashes and saw the ashes were on her head like those of a beggar and the ashes had mixed with her tears and had made mud. 19. Then Aseneth fell face-first into the ashes and stayed there until sundown. 20. She refused to eat or drink anything for seven days.

XI. Then on the eighth day Aseneth began to lose the use of her arms and legs.

XII. She looked up from the floor and reached up towards the east. She turned eyes toward heaven and she prayed,

2. "O Lord, God of all the ages, He that made everything and gave the breath of life to everything living,
that brought light to things unseen, and made things visible that were invisible,
3. That raised the sky and established the earth on the seas, that founded the huge stones on the depths of oceans so that they cannot not be submerged. Until the end of time they all follow your commands.
4. I cry out to you, O Lord, God. Hear my plea.
I confess of my sins to you and I show you my sins against your law.

5. O Lord I have sinned. I have truly sinned. I have broken your law and acted without respect or reverence toward you. And I have said evil things.

My mouth has been made unclean by praying (giving offerings) to idols, and eating things offered to idols at the tables of the Egyptians.

I valued my beauty and riches above everything.

6. O Lord, I have sinned by acting without reverence to you.

I have worshipped idols, which could neither hear nor speak.

I am wretched and not worthy to even speak to you.

7. O Lord, I, Aseneth, the daughter of Petephres the priest, have been prideful and arrogant towards you. I have valued my ancestral riches above all men.

People hate me and now they scoff at my distress.

I flee to you like a child runs to its mother and father. I pray to you and cry out to you to deliver me from my tormentors.

8. Stretch out your hands and cover me like a father that loves his children and loves them tenderly.

Pluck me now from the grasp of my enemy.

9. Look now, Lord, the wild Lion and his children chase me. They are the gods of the Egyptians that I have forsaken and spoiled. Their father the Devil is trying to devour me.

10. O Lord, you can deliver me from his grasp and deliver me from his mouth.

If you do not, he will catch me like a wolf and rip me apart.

He will throw me into a pit of fire, and into the most violent hurricane.

He will throw me into the depths of the sea.

Do not let the great monsters of the sea devour me. I will be lost forever.

11. I am deserted, O Lord. My parents have disowned me because I have broken their gods into pieces.

I now hate their gods completely.

O Lord, my only hope to be saved resides in you.

You are the father of all orphans and the champion of those who are ill-treated.

You are the aid to those who are treated unjustly.

12. I have seen that all the gods of my father Petephres are temporary and cannot be depended upon. But those who live as your heirs are eternal and live forever, O Lord.

XIII. O Lord, I am an orphan who fled to you. See my humiliation and have mercy on me.

2. Look, I have taken off my robe of royalty with gold inlay and have now put on a black tunic of mourning.

3. Look, I have taken off my gold belt and have replaced it with a rope and sackcloth.

4. Look, I ripped off the beads from my head and sprinkled ashes over myself.

5.Look, at one time the floor of my room had various colorful stones and precious purple stones all over it. The room was sprinkled with myrrh and now it is sprinkled with my tears and littered with ashes.

6. Lord, my tears have mixed with the ashes and have made mud in my room. My room looks like a well-traveled dirt road. I feel naked and afraid.

7. Lord, the dinner of fattened animals was prepared for royalty but I gave it to the dogs.

8. For seven days and seven nights I have not eaten bread or drank water. My mouth is as dry as a skin drum and my tongue looks like the horn of an animal. My lips are (cracked and broken) like broken pieces of pottery. My face is shrunken. I am going blind because my eyes have swollen from all my unceasing tears.

9. I sinned against you and said slanderous things about my lord Joseph. But I did these things in ignorance so I beg you to forgive me. I did not know that he was your son, O Lord. I am a wretch.

10. They told me Joseph was the son of a Canaanite shepherd's son and I believed them and I hated (looked down on) Joseph. I was wrong. He is your chosen one and your son but I spoke harshly to him, not knowing these things.

11. Who was ever as handsome and wise and strong as Joseph? No one but you my Lord.

I now trust him and love him more than my own soul.

12. Let him remain in your wisdom and grace. Give me to him as a servant and I will wash his feet and serve him. I will be his slave for the rest of my life.

XIV. Aseneth was completing her confession to the Lord, when she looked up and saw the morning star was rising in the sky to the east. 2. When she saw it she was overjoyed. She proclaimed aloud, "The Lord God definitely heard me because this star is a message and announces the light of a great day."

3. Then, suddenly the sky was ripped open near the morning star and a light appeared that was beyond description. 4. Aseneth bowed down with her face in the ashes as God sent a man (angel/messenger) of light down from heaven. He stood over her head and he called her by her name. "Aseneth", he said. 5. Then she asked, "Who called me? This is a high tower and the door to my room is locked. How did you get

into my room?" 6. Then he called her a second time, saying "Aseneth, Aseneth." She then answered him, "Here am I, sir. Who you are?" 7. And the man said, "I am the chief commander of the Lord, God. I am the general of all the heavenly army of the Most High. Get on your feet – stand - I will speak to you."

The angel (or heavenly man) fits the description of Michael, the archangel. Michael is mentioned three times in the Book of Daniel, once as a "great prince who stands up for the children of your people". The idea that Michael was the advocate of the Jews became so prevalent that in spite of the rabbinical prohibition against appealing to angels as intermediaries between God and his people, Michael came to occupy a certain place in the Jewish liturgy. In the vision in Daniel 10:13-21 an angel identifies Michael as the protector of Israel. Daniel refers to Michael as a "prince of the first rank." Later in the vision in Daniel 12:1 Daniel is informed about the role of Michael during the "Time of the End" when there will be "distress such as has not happened from the beginning of nations" and that: "At that time Michael, the great prince who protects your people, will arise."

In view of this, Michael is seen as playing an important role as the protector of Israel, and later of the Christian Church. The references to the "captain of the host of the Lord" encountered by Joshua in the

early days of his campaigns in the Promised Land (Joshua 5:13-15)
have at times been interpreted as Michael the Archangel,

8. When she looked up she saw he looked just like Joseph. He wore a robe and had a crown on his head and he had a staff of royalty (authority) in his hand. 9. But his face was as bright as lightning, and his eyes were like the sun and his hair was like flames. His hands and feet glowed like iron placed in a fire. Sparks flew from his hands and feet.

10. Aseneth was afraid and she began to tremble. She fell on her face at his feet in terror. 11. But the man spoke to her and said, "Be comforted, Aseneth. Do not be afraid. Stand up. I wish to talk to you." 12. Aseneth stood, and the man spoke to her, "Take off your black tunic and the sackcloth round your waist. Wash the ashes off your head and face. 13. Take a new, perfectly clean robe, never worn before, and put it on. Get two belts. Tie a bright belt round your waist – the other will signify a doubled belt of your virginity. 14. After doing these things return to me, and I will tell you what I was sent here to say."

15. And Aseneth went into her room where she kept the chests filled with her valuables and the fine things she used to adorn herself. In her wardrobe she found a new, beautiful robe. She

untied the rope and the sackcloth from her waist and took them off. She removed her black tunic and put on her new bright, clean robe. 16. Then she wrapped one belt round her waist and the other one she wrapped around her breast. It symbolized the double belt of her virginity 17. And she washed the ashes off her head and face with pure water, and covered her head with a beautiful, exquisite veil.

XV. When she came back to the divine commander and he saw her he said, "Remove the veil from your head because from this day you are a pure virgin and your head is like a young man's head."

Aseneth was always a virgin, but now she is a pure virgin, in the eyes of the angel. She is no longer simply a pagan who happens to be a virgin, but now she is a spiritual Jews and a pure virgin.

That Aseneth had "become like a young man" is a confusing statement. On the face of it, the meaning could be as simple as a "spiritual Bar Mitzvah". The Bar Mitsvah (Hebrew: בַּר מִצְוָה) and Bat Mitzvah (Hebrew: בַּת מִצְוָה)) are Jewish coming of age rituals. Bar (בַּר) is a Jewish Babylonian Aramaic word literally meaning 'son' (בֶּן), while bat (בַּת) means 'daughter' in Hebrew, and mitzvah (מִצְוָה) means 'commandment' or 'law'. Thus bar mitzvah and bat mitzvah literally translate to "son of commandment" and "daughter of commandment." However, in rabbinical usage, the word bar means "a person who is subject to the law." Although the term is commonly used to refer to the ritual itself, in fact the phrase originally refers to the person. According to Jewish law, when Jewish boys become 13 years old, they become accountable for their actions and become a bar mitzvah. A girl becomes a bat mitzvah at the age of 12 according to Orthodox and Conservative Jews, and at the age of 13 according to Reform Jews. Prior to reaching bar mitzvah, the child's parents hold the responsibility for the child's actions. After this age, the boys and girls bear their own responsibility for Jewish ritual law, tradition, and ethics, and are able to participate in all areas of Jewish community life.

The act concerning removing the veil and becoming like a young man could possibly refer to the fact that young men never wore head coverings. The Talmud also implies that unmarried men did not wear a kippah (yamaka or yarmulke: Rabbi Hisda praised Rabbi Hamnuna before Rabbi Huna as a great man. He said to him, 'When he visits you, bring him to me. When he arrived, he saw that he wore no head-covering. 'Why do you not have head-covering?' he asked. 'Because I am not married,' was the reply. Thereupon, he [Rabbi Huna] turned his face away from him and said, 'See to it that you do not appear before me again before you are married.' [Tractate Kiddushin 29b]

However, young virgin women seldom wore scarves either. Since Aseneth was 18 years of age, which would have been considered rather old to marry, we have an interesting mixed message. Was she expected to wear a veil or head covering because she was older? Was she not expected to wear one because she was a virgin and not married?

In his book on ancient head coverings, Michael Marlowe reports: Among the Greeks it seems that men did not ordinarily wear anything on their heads for worship of their gods, or in public. Generally, Greek men tended to minimize their clothing. Even nudity was not considered shameful among them in certain contexts. Because the climate in Greece is warm, men would sometimes wear nothing more than a scanty mantle called a chlamys fastened around the right shoulder, leaving the entire right side of their bodies exposed. Greek women were expected to fully cover their bodies. In the past, some biblical expositors asserted that all respectable Greek women wore head coverings, and that among the Greeks (as among the Jews) only disreputable women went about with bare heads. But there does not seem to be any good evidence for this in ancient sources. Many scholars now maintain that although Greek women certainly did wear head coverings, it was usually done in public. A woman might wear a scarf tied closely around her hair, a small shawl draped over her head (called a kaluptra, resembling the modern mantilla), or a kind of snood, called a sakkos. One statement commonly cited as evidence about the head covering customs of Greek women is in Plutarch's Sayings of Spartans (written during the first century BCE). Concerning a Spartan he writes, When someone inquired why they took their girls into public places unveiled, but their married women veiled, he said, "Because the girls have to find husbands, and the married women have to keep to those who have them!" This seems to indicate that in Sparta married women usually covered their heads in public and unmarried women did not. Many pagan religion rituals required head coverings.

In Rome, generally speaking, it was common for a woman to cover her head in public, but men wore no head covering. The Romans had a special head covering for brides, as we do today. The bridal veil was a piece of cloth called a flammeum (lit. "flame-colored"), because it was dyed bright orange, and it was draped over the bride's head without covering her face. Recently some biblical expositors have asserted that in Rome a married woman would always keep her head covered as a sign that she was married, but this assertion is not very well supported by ancient sources. The "veiling of the bride" spoken of in ancient sources pertains only to the wedding ceremony, not to a change of ordinary clothing.

Headcovering Customs of the Ancient World

An Illustrated Survey, by Michael Marlowe

2. So she took it off her head; and the angel said to her, "Be encouraged, Aseneth, you virgin. Look, the Lord has heard your confession. 3. Your name is written in the book of life and will never be blotted out. 4. Today you will be renewed, and remade, and reborn. You will eat the bread of life and drink the cup of eternal life. You will be anointed with the oil of immortality. 5. Be happy, Aseneth, you virgin. God has given you to Joseph to marry. You will be his bride and he will be your husband. 6. Your name will no longer be "Aseneth", but your name will now be "City of Refuge" because many nations shall take refuge in you. Under your wings many nations shall find shelter. All who follow God with contrition will find security. 7. Contrition is the daughter of the Most High and she pleads for you with the Most High continually as well as for all who repent. God is the father of Contrition and she the mother of virgins, beautiful and meek. Contrition, appeals to God for those who repent. Contrition prepared a bridal chamber in heaven for those who love her. She is a virgin, like them, and so she will look after them forever. 8. She is pure. She is and celibate and gentle. The Most High God loves her, and his angels admire her.

References to a "city of refuge" may be one reason some scholars believed this book to be a Christian creation. In the Old Testament, the city of refuge was a place, or group of places, where one could run to if an unintended but horrible event happened. In the New Testament the city or place of refuge becomes a person. We are told to seek refuge from the horrors and hopelessness of life in Jesus himself. Here, in the book of Joseph and Aseneth, we see Aseneth refered to as the city of refuge and her virgins as the pillars of that city.

According to the Torah, The Cities of Refuge were towns in the Kingdom of Israel and Kingdom of Judah in which the perpetrators of manslaughter could claim asylum. Outside of these cities, the law allowed blood vengeance. The Torah names just six cities as being cities of refuge: Golan, Ramoth, and Bosor, on the east of the Jordan River, and Kedesh, Shechem, and Hebron on the western side. Manslaughter, in this case, refers to the accidental or unintentional killing of a person.
We shall see that Egypt, and specifically Joseph, thus by extension Aseneth, will be the place of refuge in the coming famine. Joseph's family will come to Egypt seeking food and they will be given refuge and be saved by Joseph.

9. Now, I will go to Joseph to speak to him about you. Today he will meet you and when he sees you he will be overjoyed with you and he will marry you. 10. Aseneth, do as I say and put on the ancient wedding robe that is stored in your room and adorn yourself with your best jewelry and put on those

things a bride would wear. Make yourself ready to meet Joseph. 11. He will meet you today and he will be very happy when he sees you."

12. The angel finished speaking to Aseneth and she was overflowing with happiness. 13. She bowed at his feet and exclaimed, "Forever blessed is the Lord God because he sent you to deliver me from darkness and bring me into light. 14. May I ask you, my lord, if you would please sit down on the bed for a while, before you leave. Allow me prepare a table with bread and fine wine for you to eat and drink! Their taste will be heavenly!"

XVI. So, the man (angel) agreed to stay and said, "Please fetch me a honeycomb also." 2. And Aseneth said, "Yes sir. Let me send a servant to my parent's fields to bring you back a honeycomb." 3. But the man said, "Go into your room where you eat and there you will find a honeycomb." 4. So Aseneth went to her room and found a honeycomb lying on the table. It was full of honey. Its fragrance was like a sweet ointment and the comb was large and as white as snow.

5. So, Aseneth picked up the comb and brought it to him. Then the angel said to her, "Why did you tell me there was no

honeycomb in your house when I see you have brought me this." 6. Aseneth replied, sir, I did not have a honeycomb in my house, this thing happened just as you said. Could it have come from you, because it smells like myrrh?" 7. Then the man raised his hand and placed his hand on top of her head and said, " Aseneth, you are blessed because the hidden and indescribable mysteries of the Most High God have been revealed to you. Blessed are those who are faithful to the Lord God and contrite, for they shall eat from this comb. 8. The bees of the Paradise of Delight (which is the garden of Eden) have made this honey. God's angels eat it, and all who eat it will live forever.

9. And the man reached out with his right hand and broke off a piece of the comb and ate it. He then with his hand he placed a piece in the mouth of Aseneth. 10. Then he reached out and with his forefinger he touched the side of the comb facing east and where his finger traced on the comb the honey turned to blood. 11. Again he reached out and placed his forefinger on the edge of the comb that faced north and where his forefinger touched on the comb the honey turned to blood.

12. Aseneth was standing on the man's left side, observing everything. 13. She saw the bees began coming out of the cells of the comb. They were white as snow, and their wings

glowed with colors of purple and scarlet with threads of gold. The bees had golden crowns on their heads and sharp stringers. 14. All the bees flew in circles around Aseneth, circling her from head to foot. Then large bees, as big as queens, lit on Aseneth's lips. 15. Then the man commanded the bees, saying, "Leave and go to your places." 16. They all left Aseneth and those that intended to harm her fell to the ground and died. 17. Again the man commanded them, "Arise, and go to your place." Then the remaining bees flew up and all went to the courtyard round Aseneth's tower.

The idea of cleansing the lips or tongue and thus removing sin and even re-purposing a life is not new in the Bible. This theme occurs also in the book of Isaiah.

Isaiah 6 Holman Christian Standard Bible (HCSB) - Isaiah's Call and Mission
1 In the year that King Uzziah died, I saw the Lord seated on a high and lofty throne, and His robe[a] filled the temple. 2 Seraphim[b] were standing above Him; each one had six wings: with two he covered his face, with two he covered his feet, and with two he flew. 3 And one called to another:
Holy, holy, holy is the Lord of Hosts;
His glory fills the whole earth.

4 *The foundations of the doorways shook at the sound of their voices,*
and the temple was filled with smoke.
5 *Then I said:*
Woe is me for I am ruined[c]
because I am a man of unclean lips
and live among a people of unclean lips,
and because my eyes have seen the King,
the Lord of Hosts.
6 *Then one of the seraphim flew to me, and in his hand was a*
glowing coal that he had taken from the altar with tongs. 7 *He*
touched my mouth with it and said:
Now that this has touched your lips,
your wickedness is removed
and your sin is atoned for.
8 *Then I heard the voice of the Lord saying:*
Who should I send?
Who will go for Us?
I said:
Here I am. Send me.

In Isaiah fire is used to cleanse. For Aseneth the cleansing agent was
honey. Honey has antiseptic properties. It is one of the only foods
that does not spoil. Unless it is contaminated, honey can last for
years without spoiling.

In the story of Aseneth's "purification," honey represents the agent of cleansing. It came from a comb that was white, representing purity. The bees, being the size of queen bees, convey the idea of royalty. They lit but did not sting her. There was no harm or destruction, only purification and sanctification.

XVII. And the man said to Aseneth, "You saw this?" And she said, "Yes sir, I saw everything" 2. And the man said, "This will be the same as my command to you." 3. And the man touched the comb, and fire shot from the table through the comb and burned up the comb. As the fire consumed the comb an enlivening fragrance filled the room. It was the breath of life. 4. Then Aseneth said to the man, "Sir, there are seven virgins with me who were raised with me. They were all born on the same night as me. They serve me and I love them. Please let me call them to come so that you might bless them as you have blessed me. 5. The man replied, "Call them." So, Aseneth called them, and the man blessed them and said, "The Lord, God, the Most High, will bless you and you shall become seven pillars in the City of Refuge for ever."

6. Then the man commanded Aseneth, saying, "Remove this table." Immediately she turned to move the table but the man had vanished, but Aseneth saw something resembling a chariot of fire being lifted into the sky towards the east. 7. And

Aseneth called out, "Be merciful, O Lord, to me, your servant, because I spoke evil words in my ignorance."

XVIII. And while Aseneth was still saying these things, one of Joseph's young servants, came running up and announced, "Look! Joseph, the mighty man of God is coming to see you today." 2. And Aseneth called her servant who was over the house and said to him, "Prepare a special dinner for me, because Joseph the mighty man of God, is coming to visit us." But when the steward saw her, with her face sunken from sorrow and weeping, and fasting for seven days he wept for her and took her hand asked what was wrong. She said she had a horrible headache and could not sleep and this was the excuse she gave to the steward.

3.Then Aseneth ran up to her room and opened her wardrobe, and she took out her favorite robe. It was bright as lightning. She put it on. 4. She selected a glittering belt, made of precious stones and worthy of royalty, and she tied it around her waist. 5. Then she placed bracelets of gold on her wrists, and golden boots on her feet. She slipped an expensive necklace around her neck; and selected a golden crown with the most precious stones in it and placed the crown on her head. 6. Then she veiled herself. 7. She commanded her maid to bring pure water from the spring. 8.Then Aseneth bent down to the water in the basin to wash her face but she saw her face was like the sun, and her eyes like the rising morning star, so she stopped and did not wash, not wanting to wash away the wonderful beauty.

XIX. Then a slave, small in stature, came in and said to Aseneth, "Joseph is now at the gates of our courtyard." So Aseneth went with the seven virgins down stairs to meet Joseph. 2. When Joseph saw her, he said to her, "Come closer, you pure virgin. I have been told good things about you from heaven, and the message has explained everything about you." 3. And Joseph stretched out his arms and embraced Aseneth, and Aseneth embraced Joseph back, and they talked to each other for a long time and by their breath they received new life in their spirit.

XX. And Aseneth said to him, "Sir, come into my house." Then she took his right hand in hers and hand in hand they walked in to the house. 2. And Joseph sat down on her father Petephres's cushion. Aseneth brought in water to wash his feet but and Joseph said to her, "Tell one of your virgins come and wash my feet instead of you." 3. But Aseneth answered him, "No, sir. My hands are your hands, and your feet are my feet. No one else will wash your feet from now on." Then she did as she wanted and washed his feet. 4. Joseph took her by the right hand and kissed her and Aseneth kissed him on his forehead. 5. Then Aseneth's mother and father came back from their country estate and saw Aseneth sitting with Joseph and wearing a brilliant wedding robe. They were overjoyed and praised God and everyone ate and drank.

Joseph and Aseneth never take the left hand of the other. Always the right hand is mentioned. The right hand is the sign of power and authority. The left hand was considered an inferior side. Even today we get several words or phrases from this idea. The word, sinister, comes from the Latin word for "left". "Gauche" comes from French, meaning "left". Even the idea of getting off on the wrong foot comes from the superstition of crossing a threshold with the right foot first. Brewer tells us:

It was thought unlucky to enter a house or to leave one's chamber left foot foremost. Augustus was very superstitious on this point. Pythagoras taught that it is necessary to put the shoe on the right foot first. "When stretching forth your feet to have your sandals put on, first extend your right foot" (Protreptics of Iamblichus, symbol xii.). Iamblichus tells us this symbolised that man's first duty is reverence to the gods.

6. Petephres said to Joseph, "Tomorrow I will invite the governors and officials of Egypt, and we will celebrate your wedding, and you shall take Aseneth as your wife."

One source has Petephres giving Joseph 100 Talents of gold as a dowry. An Egyptian talent was about 60 pounds. At the present price of gold at about $1200 USD per ounce the dowry was worth about $1,152,000 (one million, one hundred and fifty-two thousand dollars). (60 pound x 16 ounces per pound = 960 ounces. 960 x 1200 = 1152000)

7. But Joseph said, " I must tell Pharaoh about Aseneth first because he is my father and he will give me Aseneth as my wife himself." 8. Joseph stayed that night with Petephres but he did not sleep with Aseneth, because he told them it would not be right for a man who worships God to have sex with his wife before their marriage."

Obviously, Pharaoh is not Joseph's biological father, but since Joseph's brother sold him into slavery and his father was told by the brothers that Joseph was dead, Joseph regards Pharaoh as a father image and Pharaoh has entrusted Joseph with his authority, just as he would have with his son. Regarding marriage rituals, in ancient cultures it was sex that established the consummation of a relationship and not necessarily a ceremony. Joseph is concerned

with carrying out things in a proper and correct order before
sleeping with Aseneth.

XXI. Joseph got up early in the morning, to send a message to
Pharaoh. He told Pharaoh all about Aseneth. 2. Then Pharaoh
sent a message telling Petephres and Aseneth to come to him.
3. Pharaoh was astonished at the beauty of Aseneth and said,
"The Lord God of Joseph will bless you, because he has chosen
you to be his bride, for Joseph is the first-born son of God, and
you will be called daughter of the Most High, and Joseph shall
be your bridegroom for ever.

4. And Pharaoh crowned them with crowns of gold and said,
5. "God Most High will bless you, He will make your family
prosperous and will give you many descendants forever." 6.
The Pharaoh turned them to face each other, and they kissed.
7. The Pharaoh came to their wedding. He issued an edict
proclaiming, "If anyone works during the seven days of
Joseph and Aseneth's wedding he shall be put to death." 8.
Pharaoh invited all the important men in Egypt. Everyone
celebrated with a banquet and drinking for seven days.

9. And when the wedding ceremony was complete and the
banquet had ended, Joseph had sex with Aseneth and she

conceived and gave birth to Manasseh and his brother
Ephraim in Pharaoh's house.

*Joseph is called "the first-born son of God." This led a few scholars to
speculate the story of Joseph and Aseneth may be an allegory of Jesus
and his bride. In this case they were not speaking of the church but of
a woman, possibly Mary Magdalene.*

*There are other explanations, which make much more sense and
follow the storyline. Joseph had proven his connection with his
Jewish God when he was able to interpret the dreams of Pharaoh and
his servants. Joseph was capable, competent, righteous, and had risen
from prison to be a ruler. In the view of the Egyptians, God was
treating Joseph like a son and Joseph was worshipping and
respecting God like a divine father.*

*There is another possibility. In Egypt, Pharaoh was a god or a
servant of god. From the second dynasty onward Pharaoh derived his
power from the sun god Ra who, by then, was the pre-eminent
creator god.*

*During the Old and Middle Kingdoms once a deceased pharaoh had
joined the gods in the skies, he was worshipped in temples adjoining
his pyramid. Ptolemy II had himself and his wife Arsinoe II deified
some two decades into his reign and was worshiped at the shrine of*

Alexander the Great at Alexandria, and all his successors did likewise after acceding to the throne. They were thought to continue to play a role as guardian deities after their death. Thus, as the son of Pharaoh, Joseph was indeed the son of god.

Joseph and Aseneth
Part Two

XXII. When the seven years of plenty ended, the seven years of famine began. 2. When Jacob heard of Joseph, he went to Egypt with his family. 3. On the twenty-first day of the second month Jacob arrived with his family and they settled in the region called Goshen within the land of Egypt.

Aseneth told Joseph, "Let us go meet your father, because your father, Israel, is my father also. Joseph answered her, "Yes, let us go together." 4. And Joseph and Aseneth went to the region of Goshen. When Joseph's brothers met Joseph and Aseneth they bowed to both of them and placed their heads on the ground. 5. Then they came to Jacob and he blessed them and kissed them. Then Aseneth hugged Jacob's neck and kissed him.

When Asenath saw him she was surprised at his beauty. His hair was white as snow and very thick and full. His white beard reached to his chest. His eyes were bright as with lightning. His shoulders and arms were shapely and his thighs and legs were large.

Jacob said to Joseph: "Is this your bride? She is blessed by the Most High God." Jacob then called her to him and blessed and kissed her. Asenath stretched forth her hands, and hugged Jacob's neck, and she kissed him.

6. Then they ate and drank together. 7. Joseph and Aseneth then left and returned to their house. Simeon and Levi escorted them, to protect them because their enemies were envious of them. Levi was on Aseneth's right hand and Simeon on her left side. 8. And Aseneth held hands with Levi because she respected him as a prophet and a man who worshipped and respected the Lord, God. Levi would see letters written in the sky, and he would read them and interpret them to Aseneth, revealing all things to her privately. Levi had a vision of her resting place, high in heaven.

XXIII. As Joseph and Aseneth were passing by, Pharaoh's eldest son was up on the wall and he saw them. 2. And when he saw Aseneth he became obsessed with her because of her beauty. Pharaoh's son sent messengers and demanded that

Simeon and Levi come to him. Then they came to him and presented themselves to him.

3. Pharaoh's son said to them, "I know that you are the best soldiers on earth. I heard it told that with your right hands you razed the city of Schechem to the ground and with your two swords you slaughtered thirty thousand men of war. 4. Now, I need your help. I wish to hire you as my companions (bodyguards – personal soldiers) and I will pay you well with gold and silver, and I will furnish you with menservants and maidservants, and provide you both with houses and larges fields (eastes) and your children will inherit them. Now, be kind to me and swear to me you will do this for me because your brother Joseph offended me because he married Aseneth and she was supposed to marry me.

5. Follow me and take up arms with me against Joseph. You will kill him with my sword, and I will marry Aseneth. For doing this you shall be counted as my brothers and my friends forever. 6. However, if you refuse my offer I will draw my sword and kill you. Then he drew his sword and showed it to them.

7. Now Simeon was a brave but rash and impulsive, so he was about to draw his sword and rush at Pharaoh's son to kill him.

8. But Levi was aware of Simeon's intention because Levi was a prophet and foresaw everything that was going to happen. So, Levi stomped down hard on Simeon's right foot as a signal for him to stifle his anger. 9. And Levi said to Simeon "Why are you so angry with him? Our father worships God, and we are his children. It is not right for those who worship God to repay his neighbor' evil acts with evil." 10. Then Levi addresses Pharaoh's son light heartedly but with respect, "Sir, why do you talk to us like this? We worship God, and our father serves the Most High God. God loves our brother, Joseph. How could we possibly do anything God would look upon as being this evil? 11. Listen, you should be careful never to let us hear of such a plan against our brother Joseph ever again. 12. If you ever try this evil plan again you will see our swords drawn against you." 13. Then Levi and Simeon drew their swords from their scabbards and said, " It was with these swords that the Lord God satisfied the rage the men of Israel had against the men of Schechem when our sister Dinah was raped, whom Schechem, Hamor's son, defiled." 14. When Pharaoh's son saw their swords were drawn, he was afraid. He began to shake and fell face first to the ground by their feet. 15. Then Levi stretched out his hand pulled him up, saying, "You need not be afraid if you are careful and never utter another word against our brother." 16. Then they left him trembling and afraid on the ground.

XXIV. Pharaoh's son was fixated on the torment caused by his desire for Aseneth, and he was grieved by his feelings. 2. His servants whispered in his ear. They said, "Look, Bilhah and Zilpah were the maidservants of Leah and Rachel, Jacob's wives and Jacob had sons by Bilhah and Zilpah. Their sons hate Joseph and Aseneth. They are jealous of them, and they will do whatever you want."

In the Book of Genesis, Zilpah is Leah's handmaid who becomes a wife of Jacob and bears him two sons, Gad and Asher. Zilpah is given to Leah as a handmaid by Leah's father, Laban, upon Leah's marriage to Jacob (see Genesis 29:24, 46:18). According to some commentators, Zilpah and Bilhah, the handmaids of Leah and Rachel, respectively, were actually younger daughters of Laban {Pirke De-Rabbi Eliezer, xxxvi.}.

According to Rashi, an 11th-century commentator, Zilpah was younger than Bilhah, and Laban's decision to give her to Leah was part of the deception he used to trick Jacob into marrying Leah, who was older than Rachel. The morning after the wedding, Laban explained to Jacob, "This is not done in our place, to give the younger before the older" (Genesis 29:26). But at night, to mask the deception, Laban gave the veiled bride the younger of the handmaids, so Jacob would think that he was really marrying Rachel, the younger of the sisters.

Zilpah also figures in the competition between Jacob's wives to bear him sons. Leah stops conceiving after the birth of her fourth son, at which point Rachel, who had not yet borne children, offers her handmaid, Bilhah, in marriage to Jacob so that she can have children through her. When Bilhah conceives two sons, Leah takes up the same idea and presents Zilpah as a wife to Jacob. Leah names the two sons of Zilpah and is directly involved in their upbringing.

Jacob
/ ---**Leah** (Reuben, Simeon, Levi, Judah, Issachar, Zebulun, Dinah)
/ --------------------**Rachael** (Joseph, Benjamin)
/--------------**Bilhah** (Dan, Naphtali)
/------**Zilpah** (Gad, Asher)

3. So Pharaoh's son sent his slave to summon these sons, and they came to meet him in the night. Pharaoh's son said to them, "I know that your are good soldiers." 4. And Gad and Dan, the elder brothers, said to Pharaoh's son, "Yes sir. We are at your service. Simply tell us what you want and we will do as you wish."

5. And Pharaoh's son was elated at their response so he told to his servants to go away and leave them alone because he had something to discuss with the men privately. 6. And all the servants left and Pharaoh's son lied to them, saying, "You have a choice between prosperity and death. Blessings and death stare you in the face right now, so choose the blessings and not death.

7. I know that you are good soldiers and that you will not die like women. Act like men and go out to meet your enemies. 8. Your brother Joseph told my father Pharaoh, that Dan and Gad are the children of maidservants and are not really his brothers. 9. Joseph told Pharaoh, "I am waiting my time until my father Jacob dies so I can take action against them and the entire families of Dan and Gad. I will make it so that they will not have an inheritance with us, because they are the children of maidservants. They are the ones that sold me to the Ishmaelites. 10. When my father is dead I will pay them back for all the wrong things they did to me."

11. And my father Pharaoh agreed with Joseph and said to him, You are correct, my son. I will assist you. So, now take the rest of my soldiers with you and go against them just as they went against you.'" 12. And when Dan and Gad heard what Pharaoh's son told them they were anxious and worried.

They said, "We beg you, sir. Help us. We are your servants and slaves. Tell us what to do and we will obey."

13. And Pharaoh's son said to them, " My father the Pharaoh acts like he is Joseph's father so tonight I will kill him. I want you to kill Joseph also, then I will marry Aseneth."

14. And Dan and Gad said to him, "We will obey your command. We overheard Joseph say to Aseneth, "Tomorrow we will go to our fields for it is harvest time. I have arranged for six hundred armed soldiers to go with you and fifty forerunners (scouts or foot-soldiers that ran ahead of the horsemen or chariots)." 15. When Pharaoh's son heard this, he gave each of the four men a battalion of five hundred men each and appointed officers and commanders over the troops.

Here it is uncertain as to who the four men are. We know two are Gad and Dan. It could be the Pharaoh's son assigned two of his men to assist Dan and Gad. It is likely Gad and Dan had their younger brothers, Naphtali and Asher with them, but soon we will discover their brothers did not agree with the deceitful behavior of Dan and Gad.

16. And Dan and Gad said to the son of Pharaoh, "We will leave in the night and hide. We will wait in the thicket of

reeds, on the bank of the brook. 17. You go ahead of Aseneth and get some distance in front of her. Take fifty archers on horseback with you. Aseneth will come right to you. Capture her. We will kill the men who are with her. 18. And Aseneth will try to escape in her chariot but she will run right into your hands and you can deal with her however you wish. 19. And afterwards we will capture Joseph while he is mourning the death of Aseneth. We will kill his children before his eyes. Then we will kill him." 20. And Pharaoh's son was delighted at what he heard, and he sent two thousand soldiers after them.

21. Gad and Dan arrived at the brook and hid in the thicket on the banks. The five hundred men with them took up their position in front of them on both sides of the road.

XXV. That night the Pharaoh's son went to his father's room to kill him with a sword, but his father's guards would not allow him to enter his father's bed-chamber. 2. And Pharaoh's son commanded them, saying, "I will see my father because I am going off to gather the grapes from my new vineyard. 3. And the guards said to him, "Your father has been in pain and awake all night long, but he is resting now. He has given us orders saying, "Do not let anyone in to me, not even my eldest son." And Pharaoh's son went away angry.

4. Then Pharaoh's son took his fifty archers on horseback, and he preceded Dan and Gad as they had told him to. 5. But Naphtali and Asher spoke to Dan and Gad asking, "Why must you plot once again to do evil against our father Israel and against our brother Joseph? You know God looks after Joseph as if he were the apple of his eye. 6. Did you not sell Joseph as a slave one day, and today he is king of all the land of Egypt? Moreover, he has saved Egypt and has given us corn. 7. If you plot against Joseph again, he will call upon the God of Israel, and the Most High will send fire from heaven to burn you up. The angels of God will fight against you." 8. But Dan and Gad, their older brothers, were angry with them, and they said, "What do you want us to do, die like women? God forbid!" And with that they departed to attack Joseph and Aseneth.

XXVI. And Aseneth got up early in the morning and said to Joseph, "I am going to our land in the country, but I am frightened in my spirit because you are not coming with me." 2. And Joseph said to her, "Be happy and do not be afraid. Go and be cheerful and do not be afraid. The Lord is with you and you are like the apple of his eye and he will keep you from all danger. 3. And I will go and distribute my corn, and give corn to all the men in the city, and no one will die of hunger in the land of Egypt."

4. So Aseneth left and started on her journey and Joseph went to distribute the corn. 5. But when Aseneth came to the brook with her six hundred men, suddenly the men that were with Pharaoh's son appeared from their ambush and engaged Aseneth's soldiers in battle, and the soldiers of Pharaoh's son killed Aseneth's men with their swords and killed all Aseneth's foot soldiers as well.

6. Then Aseneth was frightened and she fled in her chariot. 7. And Levi, the son of Leah, sensed (was informed of) all of this because he was a prophet. He told his brothers and the men of his counsel about Aseneth's danger. So they all strapped a sword to their thighs and placed their shields on their arms and picked up their spears in their right hands, and they went out after Aseneth with all the speed they could muster. 8. But, as Aseneth fled, Pharaoh's son along with fifty of his men met her, and as Aseneth saw him, and she was afraid and trembled and she called upon the name of the Lord, her God.

XXVII. Benjamin was sitting with Aseneth in the chariot on her right side. 2. And Benjamin was a strong boy, about eighteen years old, handsome beyond description (beyond the nature of men), and as strong as a young lion, and he feared God. 3. And Benjamin jumped down from the chariot, and he took a round stone that filled his hand from the brook. He hurled it at Pharaoh's son with all his might, hitting him on his left temple and wounding him severely. It was a grievous wound. He fell from his horse to the ground landing half-dead. 4. Benjamin quickly climbed up on a rock and shouted to the driver of Aseneth's chariot, "Give me fifty stones from the stream." And he gave him fifty stones.

5. And Benjamin hurled the stones. The stones pierced their temples and killed the fifty men that were with Pharaoh's son. 6. Then Reuben, Simeon, Levi, Judah, Issachar and Zebulon, the sons of Leah, pursued the men who attempted the ambush and they fell upon them suddenly, and the six of them killed all two thousand men.

7. But their brothers, the sons of Bilhah and Zilpah, fled. They said, "We shall perish here by the hands of our brothers. Benjamin killed Pharaoh's son and he is dead. All those with Pharaoh's son have perished. Six men killed two hundred and seventy-six men. Those who were left said, "Come now, let us kill Aseneth and Benjamin, then they ran into the woods with their swords drawn and covered in blood. 8. When Aseneth

saw them, and she said, "O Lord my God, who has given me life and redeemed me from the idols of corruption and death, you have said to me, 'Your soul shall live for ever', deliver me now from these men." And the Lord God heard the voice of Aseneth, and immediately the swords of her enemies fell from their hands to the ground and were became like ashes (powerless).

XXVIII. And the sons of Bilhah and Zilpah saw the amazing event that had happened and they were very fearful and cried out, "The Lord is fighting for Aseneth and against us!" 2. And they fell and bowed with their faces to the ground and were subservient to Aseneth and they said, "Have mercy on us. We will be your servants because you are our mistress and queen. Our lady we have done evil things and have wronged you and our brother, Joseph greatly.

3. God has already brought retribution upon us. We beg you to have mercy on us and deliver us from our brothers' hands, for they have become your avengers to the outrage done by us to you. Their swords are cruel and will be against us." 4. And Aseneth said to them, "Try not to worry. Do not fear, for I know your brothers are men who worship God. They do not repay evil for evil. 5. I want you to hide in the thickets until I

can quench their anger, appease them, and secure your pardon. You have dared to attempt great evil against them. 6. But try not to worry and do not be afraid, for the Lord will avenge the violence done between us. They are, after all, your father's sons. "

7. Then Dan and Gad fled to the thicket. 8. The sons of Leah came running in pursuit of them as fast as deer. But Aseneth got down from her chariot, and she greeted them with tears. 9. And they bowed to her on the ground and wept aloud. They enquired of Aseneth about their brothers, the sons of the maidservants of their father's wives, because they intended to kill them.

10. But Aseneth said to them, "Spare your brothers and do not repay evil for evil. The Lord has shielded me and melted the swords in their hands, reducing them to dust. They melted like wax in the fire. 11. The Lord is fighting for us. Isn't that enough? Therefore, spare your brothers." 12. And Simeon said to Aseneth, "Why should our mistress speak for and plead for her enemies? No! We will cut them down, kill them with our swords, because they have plotted evil on two occasions against our father Israel and our brother Joseph. Today they have plotted against you." 14. But Aseneth stretched out her hand and kissed Simeon tenderly on his check and she said to

him , "No brother, you must not repay evil for evil to your neighbor. Let the Lord avenge this violence." 15. Then Simeon bowed to Aseneth and Levi came to her and kissed her right hand, then he blessed her. 16. It was in this way that Aseneth saved the lives of those men from their brothers' anger, so that they did not kill them. But Levi knew about the men hiding in the thicket but he did not tell his brother because the wrath of Simeon and the men would have driven them to kill those hiding.

XXIX. And Pharaoh's son sat up from the ground and he spat blood from his mouth. Blood was running from his temple into his mouth. 2. Benjamin saw him and ran up to him. Benjamin took hold of the sword of Pharaoh's son and drew it from its scabbard to strike him because Benjamin did not have his own sword with him. 3. He raised the sword and was about to strike down Pharaoh's son when Levi rushed in and grabbed him by the hand and said, "No brother. Do not do this. We worship God, and it is not right for a man who worships God to repay evil for evil. It is not right to kick or injure a man who has already fallen, or destroy him in this way.

4. Instead, let us bind up his wound. If he lives he will owe us his friendship, and his father Pharaoh will be our father." 5. So Levi helped Pharaoh's son up off the ground and washed the blood off his face. He wrapped a bandage around his wounded head. Then they set him on his horse and took him to his father.

6. And Levi told Pharaoh everything that had happened. 7. When the Pharaoh heard all that was said he got up from his throne and bowed to Levi and blessed him 8. But, three days later Pharaoh's son died from the wound caused by Benjamin's stone. 9. Pharaoh mourned deeply for his first-born son, and Pharaoh was exhausted from his grief. 10. And Pharaoh died at the age of one hundred and nine. But he left his crown and his kingdom to Joseph. 11. And Joseph was king of Egypt for forty-eight years. 12. At the end of his reign Joseph gave the crown to Pharaoh's youngest, because Joseph was like a father to the child in Egypt. And Joseph praised and glorified God and he lived for years and saw the children of Ephraim.

www.ingramcontent.com/pod-product-compliance
Lightning Source LLC
Chambersburg PA
CBHW052110090426
42741CB00009B/1758